THINK SMART,
WORK SMARTER

A PRACTICAL GUIDE TO SOLVING PROBLEMS FASTER,
MAKING BETTER DECISIONS, AND IMPROVING
YOUR EFFECTIVENESS THROUGH THINKING SMARTER

ST Training Solutions
Success Skills Series

TREMAINE DU PREEZ

THINK SMART,
WORK SMARTER

A PRACTICAL GUIDE TO SOLVING PROBLEMS FASTER,
MAKING BETTER DECISIONS, AND IMPROVING
YOUR EFFECTIVENESS THROUGH THINKING SMARTER

Marshall Cavendish
Business

© 2011 Marshall Cavendish International (Asia) Private Limited
© text Tremaine du Preez
© series title Shirley Taylor
Illustrations by Edwin Ng
Cover art by Opal Works Co. Limited

Reprinted 2011

Published by Marshall Cavendish Business
An imprint of Marshall Cavendish International
1 New Industrial Road, Singapore 536196

Other Marshall Cavendish Offices
Marshall Cavendish International. PO Box 65829, London EC1P 1NY, UK · Marshall Cavendish Corporation. 99 White Plains Road, Tarrytown NY 10591-9001, USA · Marshall Cavendish International (Thailand) Co Ltd. 253 Asoke, 12th Flr, Sukhumvit 21 Road, Klongtoey Nua, Wattana, Bangkok 10110, Thailand · Marshall Cavendish (Malaysia) Sdn Bhd, Times Subang, Lot 46, Subang Hi-Tech Industrial Park, Batu Tiga, 40000 Shah Alam, Selangor Darul Ehsan, Malaysia

Marshall Cavendish is a trademark of Times Publishing Limited

National Library Board Singapore Cataloguing in Publication Data
du Preez, Tremaine,
    Think smart, work smarter / Tremaine du Preez. — Singapore : Marshall Cavendish
    Business, c2011.
    p. cm. — (Success skills series)
    Includes index.
    ISBN-13 : 978-981-4302-67-8

    1. Decision making. 2. Problem solving. 3.Professional effectiveness
    I. Title. II. Series: Success skills series (ST Training Solutions)

HD30.23
658.403 — dc22   OCN690061520

Printed in Singapore by Times Printers Pte Ltd

ACKNOWLEDGEMENTS

I am very privileged to have learnt from some great thinkers — people who have willingly shared their knowledge and passion with me over the years.

Shirley Taylor, the Success Skills series creator and editor, was prepared to give my topic a universal audience. Thank you Shirley for taking a chance on me and making this book an absolute pleasure to write. You have been a wise and inspiring companion on this journey, not only to me but also to all trainers, educators and writers who have the privilege of working with you.

The inspiration for my quest of helping the world think smart and work smarter comes from a man who doesn't need to read this book at all. My husband and friend of 12 years, Johan, the best thinker I know. No wonder I married him!

Thank you also to the team at Marshall Cavendish for bringing my manuscript to life.

Watching my little boy, Thane, grow and develop his thinking skills gives me endless pleasure as I marvel at the power and uniqueness of the human mind. I am also grateful that he is still too young to complain about me quoting his antics in this book. I won't be able to get away with that for much longer.

To Mom and Dad, Theresa, Anthony and Trevor, thank you for helping me follow every dream and run down every path that looked interesting to me. I wouldn't have found this path without each of you and my good friend, Alison Lester.

PREFACE

Congratulations on picking up this copy of *Think Smart, Work Smarter*. I'm very proud to include this in the ST Training Solutions Success Skills series. This series includes several short, practical books on a range of topics that will help you develop your skills and enhance your success at work and in your personal life too.

The Success Skills series was originally created to meet the needs of participants of ST Training Solutions public workshops. After attending our workshops, many participants expressed a real desire to continue learning, to find out more about the topic, to take it to another level. They were hungry for knowledge. Just the effect I hoped for when I set up ST Training Solutions in 2007. With the Success Skills series of books, the experience and expertise of our trainers can be enjoyed by many more people.

As Series Editor, I've enjoyed working with the authors to make sure the books are easy-to-read, highly practical, and written in straightforward, simple language. Every book is packed with essential tools and strategies that will make you more effective and successful. We've included illustrations throughout that reinforce some key points, because I believe we learn more if we add some fun and humour. You'll also notice some key features that highlight important learning points:

Myth Buster   Here you will find a statement that is not true, with notes on the true facts of the matter.

Fast Fact   Useful snippets of information or special points to remember.

Aha! Moment

This is a 'light bulb' moment, when we note something you may be able to conclude from a discussion. Don't forget to note your own 'Aha! Moments' perhaps when you receive some extra insight that clarifies an important point.

Try This

Here you'll find a suggestion for how you can put a special point into practice, either at home or at work.

Danger Zone

You'll find some words of warning here, such as things to avoid or precautions to take.

Star Tips

At the end of each chapter you'll find a list of Star Tips — important notes to remind you about the key points.

By picking up this book you have already shown a desire to learn more. The solid advice and practical guidelines provided in this book will show you how you can really go from good to great!

Good luck!

Shirley Taylor
Series Editor
CEO, ST Training Solutions Pte Ltd

www.shirleytaylortraining.com
www.shirleytaylor.com

Shape the Star in You!

Visit www.STSuccessSkills.com now to download your free e-book **'Your 7 Steps to Success'** containing motivating advice from our Success Skills authors. You can also read lots of author articles and order the latest titles in the Success Skills series.

CONTENTS

INTRODUCTION

When I began writing this book, the world was just emerging, bleary-eyed, from a financial crisis. I have now lived through three such crises. The details of each of these don't excite me, but what does are the many common threads that weave through all of them. In each of them, well-educated decision makers, with the best tools and data available, made really bad decisions that cost millions of people their savings, retirement nest eggs, jobs and dignity. These were all crises of decision making.

Spectacularly bad decisions and their owners make for sensational news stories that receive extensive media coverage. You would therefore be forgiven for thinking that only a few management decisions go spectacularly wrong and the rest are generally okay. Would you be surprised to know that, according to a study from the Ohio State University, as much as 50 per cent of management decisions go wrong?[1] If experienced, well-educated leaders and managers are making lousy decisions all the time, then so are the rest of us.

I wanted to know why this was happening and what we could all do to improve our decision-making skills. But I wasn't sure where to start. I followed many different paths in many different directions, and was fortunate enough to strike gold in many different places.

In my quest to find a decision-making process that was uncomplicated, accessible and effective, I uncovered some interesting facts. Firstly, very few people have a structured approach to thinking and problem solving. Secondly, those who do usually use complicated tools and computer programmes to help them make the best possible choices. Now don't get me wrong, there are some very smart and effective computer-based tools out there designed by people a lot smarter than me. I did my undergraduate degree in computer science and was continually impressed by the power of information systems. I am also continually surprised by how much we rely on technology and tools we don't always understand to make important decisions for us. But what about the tool that plays the most significant role in the choices that we all make — our thoughts generated by our minds?

---

1 Nutt, Paul C., *Why Decisions Fail*, San Francisco: Berrett-Koehler Publishers, 2002.

In a world of quick fixes and easy solutions, wouldn't it be great if we could pop a pill that made us smarter overnight? An instant solution to boost our brainpower may well be available one day but, until then, we have to use the tools that we already have. And that's where this book comes in. In its pages you will find useful decision-making and problem-solving ideas and tools, all presented in a clear and easy-to-apply way.

My aim in writing this book is to challenge you, to ask questions that you may not have thought of but will push you to use your thinking and decision-making tools to their limits. You may not have all the answers to the questions I ask. It's only by questioning the behaviours we take for granted and by thinking about our thinking that we can learn to be better at it.

Remember that yesterday's decisions have created your current reality and today's decisions will create your future. So join me on the road that leads to smarter thinking. If you apply the ideas and tools introduced here in your everyday life, you will soon improve the quality of your decision making, and ultimately, your career and your life. Most of all, I hope you enjoy your journey to thinking and working smarter.

Tremaine du Preez
www.leadershipconsultancy.org

ASSESS YOURSELF

What is your current understanding of decision making and problem solving?

1. Professionals with the best education always make the best decisions.

a) True

(b) False

2. When I multitask, I:

a) Get lots done, which improves productivity.

b) Impress my boss.

(c) Achieve less than I would if I did only one thing at a time.

3. If we only use 10 per cent of our brain, we can improve our problem-solving ability by:

a) Learning to access the other 90 per cent.

(b) Improving our other thinking tools, because we already use 100 per cent of our brain at different times.

c) Concentrating harder and for longer.

4. Gut feel should be ignored when making decisions.

a) True

(b) False

5. An expert in a particular field is:

a) Someone who has years of experience and can tackle any challenge with ease.

b) Someone who continually updates his or her knowledge.

c) Someone who takes risks and tries new ways to tackle new problems.

d) b and c

6. Conventional wisdom:

a) Should always be rooted out and challenged.

b) Should not be questioned because somebody already decided that it was best.

c) Is an obsolete psychological term.

7. Creative solutions:

a) Only happen to creative people.

b) Are generated through a well-structured creative process.

c) Can't be expected from a team of technical or non-creative people.

8. The best way to approach a problem is to:

a) Break it up into small pieces and analyse each one.

b) Ask what, where, when, who and why to uncover its cause.

c) Model the problem in a diagram to make sure everyone understands the problem before exploring solutions.

9. Teams always make better decision than individuals.

a) True

(b) False

10. In order to make the best decisions, I:

a) Need a comprehensive problem-solving strategy that I use every time.

(b) Need to gather every piece of information available on the topic.

c) Shouldn't give up till I find the one perfect solution, even if it means going without rest for long periods of time.

Check out these answers to see how you fared.

1. This is a myth and the answer is false. There are many factors that impact our ability to make good decisions and solve problems effectively. In Chapter 1 you'll discover that our ability to make great decisions comes from how we process information and not from our education.

2. Well done if you selected (c), because not many people do. Multitasking looks very impressive and makes us feel very useful. But ask yourself if you really get much more done this way. Chapter 2 will prove to you that we can't actually multitask at all. You'll also learn how to improve productivity with some new ideas and tools.

3. Wouldn't it be grand if we could simply unlock 90 per cent of our potential? The truth is that we actually use 100 per cent of our brain for different functions at different times. Fortunately our brain is not our only thinking tool. Chapter 3 will introduce you to your other, equally important, thinking tools and share some tips on how to use them to their full potential. The answer is therefore (b).

4. Definitely not! We tend to be a little wary of the voice in our head that jumps to very quick conclusions. Chapter 4 will help you understand why the answer to this is false. You'll learn where this voice, or intuition, comes from and how to use it wisely in decision making.

5. It would be lovely to reach a level of expertise where we can stop having to learn new things constantly. This is a tricky question to answer, so nicely done if you selected (d). An expert can easily become obsolete unless they keep taking risks and update their skills to face ever evolving and brand new challenges. Chapter 5 gives you lots of ideas on how to stay out of the expert trap. We'll also explore many other mental bloopers that trip up our best decision-making efforts.

6. The best answer here is (a). Conventional wisdom is alive and well and finds its way into our thinking surprisingly often. Challenging conventional wisdom is hard to do but it's absolutely essential if you want to make the best possible decisions or solve problems effectively. You might need a little help to do this so check out Chapter 6 on *comfort zone thinking*, where you'll learn to identify and challenge conventional wisdom.

7. If you selected (a) or (c), think again! Creativity doesn't just *happen* to anyone. Chapter 7 will walk you through a proven process to generate more creative solutions. Creative solutions are part and parcel of great problem solving, so this is an important chapter.

8. If you didn't chose (c), that's okay. Traditional problem-solving methods are still widely used but they are increasingly ineffective in dealing with the global, interconnected and complex problems we face today. Chapter 8 will discuss the latest approaches to problem solving and introduce you to a systematic way of generating solutions to your tricky problems.

9. Given that teams are so important in organisations today, you may expect the answer to be (a). Chapter 9 explores how groupthink creeps into teams and why the answer is actually (b). The symptoms of *groupthink* can be pretty destructive but there are some elegant tools to overcome it. Find out how to make your team a high performing one.

10. The answer here is (a) because a good problem-solving strategy will always help you make better decisions. Everyone has different thoughts on how to tackle problems most effectively. Throughout this book we'll uncover the myths of perfect problem solving and in Chapter 10 you'll have the opportunity to build your own problem-solving strategy.

EFFECTIVE DECISION MAKING IS VITAL FOR YOUR SUCCESS

*"Nothing is more difficult,
and therefore more precious,
than to be able to decide."*

Napoleon Bonaparte

What is your competitive advantage? Is it your education, practical training or years of working experience? Perhaps it's your product knowledge, interpersonal skills, or your ability to work longer hours than your colleagues?

If you were a professional athlete, this question might be a lot easier to answer. Professional athletes keep their bodies healthy by eating well and generally looking after themselves. They can spend up to 10 hours a day refining their skill — doing the same thing over and over till they get it just right. They review their performance, study their competitors and develop the mental mindset of a champion. The amount of time they actually spend in competition is very little compared to the time spent preparing for it. They work *on* their game more than they work *in* the game. Depending on the discipline, their competitive advantage is to be better, faster or stronger than their competitors.

As professional knowledge workers, we are not so different from professional athletes. Those who excel in business develop their competitive advantage by working *on* their profession as much as they work *in* it. What then is this competitive advantage that those at the top of their game have developed? Quite simply, it's their minds. Their ability to think faster and smarter allows them to work smarter, make better decisions and be rewarded for it.

The rest of us tend to live *in* our game. We work long hours and have to keep looking ahead to the next meeting, project or sale. Yet we are also expected to be better, faster and smarter than our competitors. So we nourish our minds with education. We learn stuff about stuff and gather more facts than we could probably use in one lifetime. While I don't underestimate the value of information as the building blocks of good thinking, facts alone seldom help us develop our mind's full potential as our competitive tool.

Fast Fact

Facts are the building blocks of decision making but simply knowing lots of facts won't make you smart.

Key benefits of making good decisions

Every single action that we take or don't take throughout our lives is a direct result of a decision. Wherever you are today is the result of all the decisions that you have made in your life.

In the same way, companies fail or succeed based on all the decisions made by their leaders, managers, support staff, front-line staff and even their suppliers' staff. The quality of all these decisions depends on the quality of the thoughts that produce them.

Aha! Moment

Where I will be in the future depends on the decisions I make today for myself, my family and my career.

Even when we feel we don't have a choice, as we so often do, we always have the choice not to decide, say or do anything. I have a three-year-old son, and for him the most crucial decision in his life right now is deciding when to go to the bathroom. He tries to time it just right so that he doesn't miss out on too much play or the best part of a TV programme. Sometimes he decides not to decide, and this decision has rather wet consequences.

It's no secret that a child's attention span is as long as his decision-making time horizon. Whatever brings instant reward is the first choice. My son is no different. At the moment, teaching him to be aware of the consequences of his decisions is as effective as explaining to him that candy has no nutritional value and is best left on the shelf! Fortunately, with practice, we get much better at making the basic decisions. As we get older our decisions get somewhat more complicated than which part of *Mickey Mouse Clubhouse* to miss out on. Unfortunately, we don't get nearly enough practice with the hardest of decisions, and we don't get immediate feedback that allows us to see where we went wrong or right, until it's too late.

How to tell good decisions from bad ones

Think of some of your past decisions and ask yourself which ones worked out really well for you. Chances are they all had something in common. The same probably applies to those decisions that didn't turn out so well.

Let's take a look at some of the similarities you may find in your more successful decisions:

- You weren't expected to make a decision on the spot (although every now and again a quickie does work out okay!)

- The decision had a very clear goal or purpose, and you knew what that was.

- You understood exactly what your options were and had time to research them.

- You were able to verify the information that you used to help you make your decision.

- You asked for input from other people whose opinions you respect.

- You received some opinions that didn't agree with yours and didn't disregard them.

- You spent time reflecting on the possible positive and negative outcomes of the decision.

- If you had a really strong *gut feel* about something, you took the time and effort to try to understand why.

- The outcome of your decision didn't rely on events beyond your control, other people or luck.

This is by no means an exhaustive list of the qualities of great decisions, but I'm sure you recognised some of these in the decisions that turned out well for you. On the other hand, you may recognise that many of these were missing from the decisions that didn't turn out so well.

Some of the similarities you may find in your not-so-smart decisions may be:

- You felt you were under pressure to make a decision quickly.

- You made a snap judgment.

- Unchecked emotions played a large part in your final decision.

- You were surprised by the outcome of your decision.

Myth Buster

Surely it's purely coincidence or bad luck if we sometimes repeat the same mistakes in our decision making.

Think again! Every one of us has a decision-making process. If your decisions often turn out poorly or if you repeat the same mistakes, those mistakes may actually be due to your decision-making process.

I'm well educated, so I must be smart

If the 1980s and 1990s were the age of management and management education, the 21st century has so far been the age of leadership and leadership education. Today's leaders are trained in hard and soft skills, such as emotional intelligence and coaching — topics that would have seemed inappropriate in the age of tough management. Today, leaders are well-educated, have unprecedented access to information and decision-making tools, and can increasingly tap into the minds of great thinkers and strategists through global connectivity. Why is it then that 50 per cent of all management decisions go wrong in one way or another?

Fast Fact

Being really well-educated and using *proven* decision making tools is not helping decision makers to make better decisions every time.

It seems that being educated certainly makes one well-informed, but not necessarily smart. How, then, can leaders improve their smarts and make better decisions on behalf of workers and citizens everywhere? And can anyone learn the skills of being smart, or is it something we are gifted with from birth?

I'm not well educated, so I can be smart

The good news is that becoming a good thinker and making great decisions is a skill that can be learnt just like learning a foreign language. Don't worry if you find learning a foreign language daunting. The language of smart thinking and decision making doesn't require you to learn many words nor grapple with various tenses. The secret lies in how often you practise it.

Some of the smartest thinkers of our time, who have generated breakthrough ideas and top-notch decisions, would be considered undereducated by today's standards. Bill Gates, Steve Jobs and even Henry Ford dropped out of college, while other leaders such as Sir Richard Branson and Winston Churchill didn't even attend college. In fact, Thomas Edison was home-schooled till the age of 12, when he joined the railways. These men, and thousands of other men and women like them, are considered to be great thinkers despite their lack of formal education. Their decisions weren't always orthodox or based on principles taught in textbooks, but they were able to make better decisions, on average, than many of their contemporaries.

In order to understand how to make great decisions, we need to understand exactly what decisions are. Read these six words and phrases and place a tick beside the ones that you think best describe the activity of decision making:

❑ Cognitive   ❑ Emotional

❑ Rational   ❑ Irrational

❑ Based on proven facts ❑ Based on assumptions

If you ticked the three on the left, you would be describing what we would all like decision making to be and what traditional decision-making theory, found in economics textbooks, says it is. If you ticked the three on the right you would be describing the traditionally accepted components of decision making. If decision making lurks in the world of the emotional and irrational, then this would explain why decisions go wrong for even the best educated. However, it's not all bad news, because now that we know why decision making and problem solving goes wrong, we can take steps to fix it.

 Myth Buster

I need to learn how to remove emotions from my decision making because the best decisions are based solely on logic and reason.

Not so! An initial, emotional response underlies every decision we make, and we couldn't make any decisions without them. It is not possible to remove emotions from our decision making. Rather, learn how to identify and harness any harmful impact that emotions could have on our judgment.

If you still firmly believe that decision making lives in the realm of the rational and logical, then jump on over to Chapter 3 where we explore emotions in decision making. You'll be glad you did.

Find out what type of decision maker you are

Every one of us is unique and has a very special personality that has been developed over our lifetime. Your personality has been shaped by your cultural heritage, your upbringing and personal experiences. In the same way, your decision-making style is unique to you. It's the same for everyone else.

Have you ever thought about what your decision-making style is? Perhaps you've commented on someone else's decision or actions by saying, "Well, I would have done it differently," or "That wouldn't have been my choice." But what are the steps that you take when you are faced with alternatives? Do you gather opinions and discuss your options with close friends and family, or do you research your ideas and make a unilateral decision? Are you the type who makes decisions on the spot or do you stew over all your options until you run out of time? Maybe you prefer not to make any decisions at all?

Personalities can be profiled and grouped into broad categories. This helps us understand how to manage and motivate ourselves and others. In the same way, decision-making styles can be grouped into broad categories. Understanding the way we make decisions, on average, will help each of us to pick out the flaws in our process and improve how we approach every decision that comes our way.

Quiz: What's your dominant style?

Circle the option a, b, c or d that applies most closely to you.

1. When I go for lunch with a group of friends, I...

a)   suggest a new eating place that I saw advertised.

b)   ask everyone to suggest their favourite restaurants and see which one is most popular.

c)   research food blogs to find good restaurants in the area.

d)   ask someone else to pick the restaurant.

2. Roadworks in your area are making you late for work every day. You...

a)   try different routes to see which one works best.

b)   use the same route and wait it out; traffic will eventually get better.

c)   use Google Maps to find a better route.

d)   ask your neighbour how he gets to town and use his route.

3. A new gym has opened up really close to your home and your old gym membership is expiring. You...

a)   join the new gym immediately to benefit from the early bird special.

b)   take too long to think about it, miss the early bird special, so stay with your old gym because it's less hassle that way.

c)   schedule an appointment to meet the membership officer and research opinions online.

d)   join the new gym because a good friend has joined (although he hasn't been yet, so can't give you any feedback).

4.   You are responsible for arranging your company's annual conference. You...

a)   try a different venue that hasn't been used before because they offer a great package.

b)   invite venue operators to submit proposals and brochures, and review them carefully.

c)   visit several venues and compare their packages before deciding.

d)   use the same venue that was used last year, even though it is more expensive than some of the others.

5.   You have made a decision and somebody you respect disagrees with you. You...

a)   listen to their reason but defend your opinion.

b)   tell them you'll think about it and feel confused as to what is the right choice.

c)   research their opinion and decide if it's valid or not.

d)   go along with their suggestion.

6. You prefer your work environment to be...

a)   flexible where no two days are the same.

b)   relaxed with long-term projects and no immediate deadlines.

c)   supportive with guidelines that you are allowed to use or change.

d)   structured with set daily activities and standard operating procedures.

7.   You have a light headache that keeps recurring. You...

a)   keep trying different headache tablets.

b)   use the same tablets and hang in there till it goes away.

c)   see your GP.

d)   see a neurologist.

8.   You prefer to work...

a)   with different people all the time.

b)   with the same group of colleagues for many years.

c)   wherever you get offered the most attractive package.

d)   in the same job for many years.

9.   When faced with a critical decision, you...

a)   decide quickly and by yourself.

b)   wait for as long as possible before making your decision.

c)   systematically evaluate all your alternatives and gather opinions.

d)   refer to an expert to make the decision for you.

10.   Your car breaks down on the highway. You...

a)   open the bonnet and 'fiddle' till it starts up again.

b)   wait till the traffic police drive past and help you.

c)   call a 24-hour breakdown hotline.

d)   call a friend to help you out.

Scoring:

Count up how many you scored of each letter and then check out the major characteristics of your dominant style below:

A: _2_

B: _2_

C: _5_

D: _____

A: Spontaneous style

To be spontaneous is a gift, sometimes. Many of us are spontaneous in our youth but grow increasingly cautious over time, every time our fingers get burnt. If you scored more A's you tend to have a spontaneous decision-making style, you are probably comfortable making decisions *on the spot* and are guided by intuition and what *feels* right. You are happy to accept a trial-and-error approach to your mistakes and successes, and usually have a conscious or unconscious confidence in your decision making. Remember not to confuse this style with the confidence that comes from many years of experience in a particular field, where decisions appear to be spontaneous but are actually just taken at lighting-fast speed because the brain is already primed.

B: Delaying style

On the other end of the spectrum are those who couldn't imagine making a spontaneous decision or going along with gut feel. If you scored more b's, it seems you prefer to delay making a final decision for as long as possible. This allows you to gather as much information as possible to make sure that you don't miss any valuable facts that could change the outcome of your decision. The belief that there is always more information available can lead to you lacking confidence in your decisions. People who delay finalising decisions would be considered careful and considerate but perhaps also hesitant decision makers.

C: Systematic style

In the middle of the spectrum lies the ideal decision maker. Ideal in many respects, but not all. If you scored more c's, you tend to have a systematic process that kicks in every time you are faced with having to make important decisions. You probably seek out many alternatives and evaluate them in a systematic way. If this sounds like you, this process can create a level of comfort and confidence in your judgment. However, there is also a danger here in that you may become over-reliant on this process, and may not be able to adapt it as circumstances change, which they invariably do.

D: Referring style

For others, making decisions can be a truly nerve-wrecking exercise. If you scored more d's you may prefer not to make any important decisions at all. Do you refer decisions to others, friends, family members, colleagues or experts (perceived or real)? This is not because you don't have ideas or opinions; on the contrary, you probably have great ideas but prefer not to voice them. This happens for many reasons — personal, religious, political or cultural.

Now, take a minute to think of the biggest financial decision you ever made. A large investment in property or the stock market, buying the family car or something more racy, your education or your children's education? Even the decision to have a child is partly an economic one. What was the process that you used?

My husband and I have just decided to have a second child. Did we look at our balance sheet, price schools or look at bigger apartments before we made our decision? Nope, we decided that our three-year-old son would be much happier with a sibling than a puppy. Like most people, we made perhaps the second-biggest financial and emotional commitment that we could make (after deciding to have our first child) based on how we felt as parents and an emotional desire to expand our family. This is okay. Having a family will always be an emotional decision because, whichever way you look at it, raising children may not make financial sense but it does *feel* right.

Star Tips for boosting your decision-making confidence

1. Give yourself a high-five for having picked out a book on thinking and decision-making skills.

2. Remember that, as a knowledge worker, your ultimate competitive advantage is your mind's ability to think thoughts that are faster and smarter than your colleagues and competitors.

3. Don't feel that a lack of education means that you can't make great decisions. Some of the best decision makers of our time had no formal college education.

4. Don't think that a fantastic education automatically means that you can make great decisions. Great decisions come from how we deal with information that challenges us, especially if we have never encountered it before.

5. Calculate how much time you devote to thinking about thinking and developing your ability to think smarter and work smarter. Is it enough?

6. Get to know your decision-making personality by examining your decision-making style.

7. Think about past decisions that you've made. Did the more successful ones have something in common?

8. Examine your less successful decisions; do you seem to be repeating the same mistakes?

9. Recognise that the quality of your life depends on the quality of the decisions that you make.

10. Make today count by acknowledging that where you will be in your future depends on the quality of your thoughts plus the decisions you make today.

GETTING ON TOP OF INFORMATION OVERLOAD

2

"You could read 5,000 pieces of content and find what you want. But usually you want to do some other things with your life."

Barak Hachamov

As a teenager growing up in Africa, I vividly remember waking up early on Saturday mornings feeling sleepy, lazy and not looking forward to the day. Every month we would have to complete work for one of our school projects. Our neighbourhood library wasn't open on Saturday afternoons or Sunday, so project work ate up my Saturday mornings. I still smile when I think back to all the memories of catalogue cards, hardcover volumes wrapped with thick plastic, and teenagers trying to stifle their giggles. I also remember photocopying pages from encyclopaedias and then rewriting information — by hand. You are probably thinking that I must be very old, but I'm not!

 Fast Fact

Technology is rapidly changing our relationship with information. We used to have to *go to* information during office hours. Now it comes to us — 24 hours a day, seven days a week.

The American author of *Data Smog*, David Shenk, summed it up perfectly when he wrote, "Information, once rare and cherished like caviar, is now plentiful and taken for granted like potatoes."

Apart from the ease and abundance of our relatively new, information-rich culture, there are also frustrations and challenges. But first let's take a look at why we love having unlimited access to information.

There are the obvious reasons, such as not having to spend a perfectly good sunny Saturday morning in complete silence at the library. Now we google, yahoo or baidu from the comfort of our home — or anywhere for that matter.

Our love of information can be likened to our love of food. We need a certain amount and variety to stay healthy and informed. If we have just enough, we feel well and in control of our diet and health. If it is beautifully presented, it appeals to our senses. If it is sweet and satisfying, we might just want a second or third helping. Too much information, like too much sticky toffee pudding, will leave us feeling bloated and unable to digest it all.

We also love information because it increases our confidence in our decision-making abilities. If a little information helps us make informed decisions, more information must be better, right? Well let's see. Handicappers at horse races rely on information to make accurate predictions about which horse is going to win the race. Having more information than other handicappers would certainly lead to better decision making. But hold on, research shows that handicappers with 40 pieces of information made predictions that are no better than those with five pieces of information.[2] What did change, however, was their confidence in their decisions, like the sugar rush that comes from eating too much candy. There is a point at which information confuses and derails our thinking, leaving our decision-making ability worse off.

---

2   Slovik, Paul. *Behavioral problems of adhering to a decision policy.* 1973. Available at www.decisionresearch.org/people/slovic

Myth Buster

The more information I can gather, the better my decisions will turn out.

Not always! There is a point at which too much information actually causes a deterioration in our decision-making abilities.

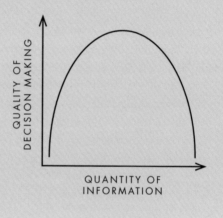

Has the term *information overload* already sprung to mind? These two words don't simply refer to the presence of too much information in your Inbox, or the mind-boggling array of data tangled up in the World Wide Web. According to futurist Alvin Toffler, 'information overload' refers to the difficulty we can have understanding an issue and making decisions, caused by having too much information.

Fast Fact

The term *information overload* actually refers to the negative effect that too much information has on our ability to understand an issue.

Information overload is a virus that we will all be infected with at various points in our lives. Unlike flu or chicken pox, no vaccination can prevent it and no pill can make us better. Information has to be constantly managed and disciplined, like our affection for food. I'll share some ideas on how to do that in just a minute, but first we need to investigate your relationship with information. Do you nibble at it like a mouse or do you devour every last piece until your brain hurts?

What is your information diet?

Are you fully aware of the role that information plays in your life? Are you always connected to an information source? Let's audit your information diet. Over one full weekday, take note of how much information you consume using the table on the next page. Every time you request or receive information, record it in the table. This can include receiving and responding to e-mail and text messages, web surfing, Facebooking, reading printed media, watching the news on TV, your computer, iPad or reader, or any other electronic information source specific to your company or job. Gossip doesn't count! Try not to skip the last column.

Information source	Number of minutes or hours per day?	Business or pleasure?	How much was truly productive?
Total for the week			

Very often we turn to a search engine to research one very specific issue. We specify our query perfectly and are rewarded with several hundred sites that have exactly the information we need. So far so good. But what happens then? Do you, like me, often fall prey to the seductive links and flashing banners that lure us down all sorts of paths away from our ultimate goal? It's a virtual conspiracy indeed.

We have come to accept that information on the Internet is largely free of charge. Does this ever prompt you to wonder how the people providing this free information earn their money? They earn it by advertising or promoting products or special offers that *do* generate a fee. Just like the chocolate bars and candy that line the checkout counter at your supermarket, information is strategically placed on websites inviting you to follow one link and then another and then… oh dear. Have you ever bought a chocolate bar that you really didn't need? How often have you been carried away and wasted a great deal of time thinking that the information you were chasing may just be useful, but it wasn't?

So when you fill in the last column of your information diet, think about how much time you spend on the Internet, or reading a magazine or newspaper. For how much of this time are you able to stay focused on your ultimate objective without getting distracted?

Information has to be constantly disciplined. We have to set our own information boundaries and only accept information that truly adds value to us. Much like choosing wholegrain crackers to snack on instead of candy!

Myth Buster

I stay informed by subscribing to newsletters, podcasts, blogs and newspapers. I can't possibly read everything, but if I need the information at least I know I have it available somewhere.

If you agree with this, your information diet could be doing you more harm than good. You may be overloading yourself with information that could easily be called up by searching for it on the Internet when you need it.

Try This

Try subscribing only to information sources that you actually have the time to read and enjoy. You won't have the chance to feel overwhelmed and stressed by everything you never get around to reading.

How much is enough?

There is no right answer here, only a wrong one. When I ask my workshop participants this question, they often reply, "We can never have enough information!" I disagree. We certainly can. In fact, we are often exposed to way too much, which ultimately leads to information fatigue. When we can't live without our e-mail or daily Facebook fix, we venture into the world of information addiction. Don't be alarmed by the thought of being an addict. I can't reach 10 am with a smile on my face and a clear head unless I've had my shot of coffee! Does that make me a coffee addict? Probably, but it doesn't affect my productivity or my ability to make decisions. When it does, I'll worry. Given the sheer amount of information coming at us at the same time all the time, however, it may be time to worry.

On top of that, how many magazines, periodicals, industry publications, newspapers, newsletters, news alerts, blogs, weekly updates, tweets, Facebook notes, RSS feeds, LinkedIn group updates or YouTube channels (and all the others I've missed out) do you subscribe to? Another cause of information fatigue, and a great deal of de-motivation and frustration, is caused by information that we have asked for, yet end up drowning in.

If I'm honest, I already have trouble reading one business magazine a month along with a quarter of the daily paper, Bloomberg updates, the evening news and one or two business books. Novels are strictly for holidays. On my desk there is a pile of unopened Harvard Business Reviews glaring at me. I definitely want to read them all one day because they contain loads of valuable ideas, plus I paid for them! Every morning my Inbox is jammed with *indispensible ideas from thought leaders and others* that I subscribe to through various sites. When faced with this much information first thing in the morning, I get a real buzz, but by mid-morning I've achieved little and I'm not much smarter. Instead, I'm already feeling tired! Remember that a messy or crammed information diet will bog anyone down.

"One Sunday [1998] edition of the *New York Times* carries more information than the average 19th century citizen accessed in his entire life."

— WILLIAM VAN WINKLE

So how much is enough? Just as everyone has different calorie and dietary requirements based on our level of activity, body mass and metabolism, so each of us will have different information requirements and tolerance. When you start noticing any of the symptoms of information overload from the next section, it might be time to think about cutting some information candy out of your daily information diet.

The effects of information overload

I love 'almost full' parking lots. My heart sinks when I drive into the car park at my local supermarket and I am faced with 70 open lots. I drive around and around looking for the perfect place to park Hillary, our family car. I find fault with every bay near me and feel sure there will be a better one just on the other side. However, if there are only five or even ten lots available, the first one I see is always a great choice. The same goes for spaghetti sauce. Why can't I just have three options to choose from instead of the 23 that stare at me from the shelves at 5 pm on a Friday afternoon — when I am incapable of making *any* kind of decision? Does this ever happen to you?

Information overload can affect our reasoning, judgment and physical health. As a business coach, I see many of its effects first hand. My clients usually tell me they are either overworked, stressed, tired, have a demanding boss, spouse or family, or haven't had a holiday in ages. Very few think they suffer from information overload, until they examine their information diet.

Do you experience any of these on a regular basis?

- A quickening heart beat and rise in blood pressure when you think about a project or even just your workday.

- A feeling of being constantly overwhelmed, confused or frustrated.

- A deterioration in your ability to make decisions.

- Being taken aback by the outcomes of your decisions when you were really sure that you had made the right choice.

- A struggle to wind down at the end of the day and interact with other people face-to-face in a friendly way.

- A general inability to connect with other people face-to-face. You may even try to avoid being in a position where you have to do so. Have you ever been to a networking event and spent almost the whole time texting or checking your e-mail?

- Going to bed with the day's information swimming around in your head. Do you battle to fall asleep because you are still generating ideas way after bedtime?

 Fast Fact

According to David Shenk, author of *Data Smog*, the typical business manager is said to read one million words per week. If a full-length novel is 90,000 words, managers are reading 11 novels a week and just over two novels in a workday.

Is that even possible? We may be exposed to this much information but our brains cannot make sense of it all. There is a point in the decision-making process where more information leads to an increase in confusion.

In our house we have an ongoing debate on whether or not dairy products are good for an adult. I think they are fine, and I have found plenty of research to support that fact; not to mention my love for frothy, milky lattes. Others in the house believe that dairy products are harmful, with equal amounts of research to back this up, and support a preference for neat espressos. The massive amount of free information available on the topic has twisted and confused our decision making and could be affecting our health in the long run.

 Try This

If you experience any of the symptoms of information overload or just feel giddy when you think of the information in your world, then try this: start culling information from your life until you reach a point where you feel 100 per cent in control of your information diet.

Information unload

It's okay not to read everything in the newspaper and not to stay on top of the day's news as it unfolds (it's just going to change tomorrow anyway) and to limit newsletters to only one or two a week. My job doesn't rely on being on top of the news as it unfolds. Some time ago, I switched from receiving daily news, which is usually quite messy and noisy, to weekly news. A reliable information source that sums up the week's news, with perhaps a bit of intelligent commentary that puts it all in perspective, is a much calmer, clearer and smarter choice. If something really important happens in the world, you'll know about it. I heard about a volcano that erupted in Iceland, causing severe air traffic disruptions, within minutes of the official announcement, without having access to any form of daily news, because everyone was talking about it. Of course, this only works if your job doesn't rely on you being up-to-the-minute on current global events. If you subscribe to an industry specific news service or even a cut-down news service such as Reuters, you'll get only that which is most important to you, without being bombarded.

 Aha! Moment

If I don't really need to stay up-to-the-minute on global news, replacing daily information sources with weekly summaries and commentaries will give me a much clearer picture of global events without all the noise and sensationalist details.

Here are some ideas to help you deal with the mind-boggling amount of information that we are exposed to every day.

- Information is no longer power, and it certainly doesn't give you the professional edge because everyone has access to the same information.

- Information should be treated as raw data. Our edge is in how we make sense of it all through thinking critically and creatively about it.

- A good dose of scepticism is essential when browsing free data.

- Find and use trusted, good quality sources of information. Browsing web pages that have lots and lots of attractive links and advertisements is a sure way to get distracted and waste time.

- Schedule specific times every day to read information that is critical to your job. If you must do this at your desk, ask your computer to sleep or close your browser — this is not e-mail time.

- Use information filters such as a junk mail filter, and be very careful about adding your e-mail address when making online purchases or visiting new sites.

- Avoid random sampling of information. Try to have an action plan when looking for information online. Stay focused and don't let yourself get distracted by attractive banners or suggestions.

- Have a clear distinction between entertainment time online and work or research time online, and don't allow the lines to blur.

Here is another suggestion that may seem rather radical at first. Feel free to dismiss it. However, if you truly want to get back control of your information diet, read on.

Set specific and limited times for various information sources and repetitive work. For example, checking your e-mail once every hour at 15 minutes to the hour will leave you with 45 minutes of uninterrupted work time. Of course, it's even better if you can check your e-mail a maximum of two or three times a day. This suggestion tends to cause disbelief from participants on my training programmes. The truth is that it can be done, but we are so terrified of missing out on something super important, something that could change the course of history, that we stay slaves to the ping or the pop-up of our mailbox.

What happens just after we reach for our phone or open our mailbox to pounce on a newly-arrived message? Usually we read it and then flag it for later or mark it as *unread*. We are often not in a position to send an immediate reply or to action a message, but we still allow ourselves to be disrupted just to read it.

Go on, pick a day where you check your e-mail at regular intervals only. It's liberating, although perhaps a bit nerve-racking at first. It puts you straight back in control of your daily agenda. Information is no longer power, controlling it is.

Create a bin list

To-do lists come in various shapes, sizes and levels of complexity — from stuff in your head to notes scrawled on the back of a till slip to elaborate GTD (getting things done) systems and project management flow charts. To-do lists are useful and necessary. They keep us focused on what we have to do next, how much we have to do and by when.

On the flip side, to-do lists can sprout like weeds. How many do you have in your life right now, as you are reading this? If we don't spend time actively managing and pruning these lists, they can go from being a tame terrace garden to a wild forest in no time at all.

Do you have items on your to-do list that have been there for longer than six months? A to-do list that never seems to get shorter, or has items on it that you never seem to get around to, is extremely de-motivating. Like clothes that we haven't worn for two years that still hang in our closet taking up unnecessary space, we find it hard to take things off our to-do lists. If it's been there for six months, it may be time to accept that it will never be done, or isn't critical enough to demand your immediate attention. Perhaps it's time to remove it from your list? If the item is really important, it will find its way back onto the list, perhaps with some urgency next time.

There may also be things in your life that you still do but that have become unproductive or unrewarding. I used to go to all sorts of different professional interest group meetings, hoping to generate new business. This took up a lot of time. When I finally did an audit of where my new business was coming from, I discovered — after two years of going to these meetings — that only a few of them had generated any business for me. It's the 80/20 principle in practice. I received 80 per cent of my business from 20 per cent of my networking. This insight made me drop the unproductive meetings and focus my energy where it was most rewarded.

Many of us are so busy focusing on what we should be doing that we never cull daily activities that have become unproductive. The more we stop doing, the more time we have for the stuff we really want to do and should be doing.

 Aha! Moment

If I spend 15 minutes less on Facebook or other social media every day, it will give me at least an extra hour with my friends, loved ones or family at the weekend.

We can't multitask but we try

> **Personal Assistant to CEO urgently required**
>
> Must be willing to travel with CEO, work long hours and remain calm under pressure. Built-in networking abilities, full multitasking functionality and a pleasant disposition are essential for success in this demanding role. Apply within.

Does this CEO need a PA or a PC?

The term multitasking is an invention of the computer age. It didn't exist before that. A true multitasking machine has two processors that can perform in parallel. If a human being was born with two processors they would be whisked into surgery to correct this anomaly.

While top performers pride themselves on their ability to multitask, we actually don't have two processors at all. Any additional activity that we perform takes resources, or processing power, away from the current activity. Not only can we really not do two things at the same time (not with 100 per cent accuracy anyway), we also can't chop and change between activities without impairing our ability to do them well.

On your next working day, count how many times you are interrupted and your attention is taken away from the activity you are working on. This number will probably surprise you. How long did it take you to regain the initial level of concentration that you were enjoying before the interruption? For many people it can be up to 15 minutes. Multiply that by the number of times you get distracted every day and the answer will explain why there are some days when you achieve very little, despite feeling really busy.

So how come we can shower and sing, walk and chew, watch TV and eat? This is because these are unconscious activities. When an activity is repeated frequently enough, our unconscious mind takes charge of it and we don't actually need to 'think' about what we are doing. We don't do most of our daily work activities nearly enough to perform them unconsciously. Two pilots of a commercial jet airliner had a different opinion though and thought they could catch up on e-mails while flying an aeroplane. Not even pilots with 31,000 hours of flight experience between them, who were not suffering from fatigue, could multitask on the job.

October 27, 2009

(CNN) — The pilots of the commercial jetliner that last week overshot its destination by about 150 miles have said they were using their laptops and lost track of time and location, federal safety officials said Monday.

Myth Buster

We live in a world where we are expected to multitask. If I can't multitask, I will be uncompetitive.

Think again! Multitasking actually reduces personal efficiency, damages productivity and hurts morale. The ability to multitask doesn't make you a more valuable employee.

Unitasking

Is there a solution to the limitations of multitasking? Yes. Unitasking. As the name suggests, unitasking involves doing one thing at a time, using all our mental ability to focus on the task at hand. Although unitasking makes you more productive, it might not be a good idea to declare your amazing ability to unitask at your next job interview!

The misperception that we should be able to do two things really well at the same time will persist for some time yet. However, if you try unitasking, I know you will notice better returns to your daily work effort, better idea generation and a much more productive workday.

Star Tips for taking control of your information diet

1. 'Take the best and leave the rest' is good practice when browsing the web for information. Only use good quality sources of information where possible.

2. Remember that electronic information is not knowledge. It should not replace reason, judgment and good old-fashioned thinking.

3. Use electronic information as raw data to form your own ideas.

4. Track your information diet and look for signs of information overload.

5. Unsubscribe from sources of information that you aren't able to read regularly. If you need this information in the future, it will still be there on the Internet and you can simply search for it.

6. Start a 'not-to-do' list to help you cull those activities that you should no longer be doing because they have become unproductive.

7. Scale back on activities that you do too much of. You will have more time to do the things you really want (and need) to be doing.

8. Keep track of how often you are interrupted during your workday and notice the effect it has on your productivity.

9. Try to work uninterrupted for short periods of time and set specific times to check mail and do other repetitive tasks.

10. Unitask wherever possible.

MAKING THE MOST OF YOUR PERSONAL THINKING TOOLS

"An interest in the brain requires no justification other than a curiosity to know why we are here, what we are doing here, and where we are going."

Paul D MacLean

Some years ago I worked for a large investment company and drove a Volkswagen. I loved my Volkswagen. I parked it in the same, assigned, parking bay every day of the week and on some weekends too. After one particularly bad day at the office, I climbed into my VW, fuming over a heated debate I'd had with a colleague, and I reversed straight into a pillar. My first thought was, "What? A pillar? When did they build a pillar there?" (Actually my *very first* thought was a word my editor won't let me publish!) I was sure a pillar hadn't been there the day before. But I was wrong! It had actually been there ever since the parking lot had been constructed some 15 years earlier; I had just never noticed it. How bizarre. Unfortunately, my insurance company didn't share in my surprise.

I managed to put this event out of my mind for some time until a related, but far more serious, incident happened. In the weeks after our son was born, I decided to resume my usual morning walks along the pier of the marina near our apartment in Hong Kong. Surely this would be a lovely outing for my new bundle of joy? So I left the house early one morning listening to the birds and enjoying the still morning air. After a few minutes I had a nagging feeling that something was missing. I brushed this aside and continued to enjoy the view of the South China Sea as I approached the pier. Then I realised what was missing — my baby!

Safely fast asleep in his cot with his nanny bustling around downstairs, my little bub was none the wiser, but I was. It certainly can't be the first time a new mom has done something like this, but I couldn't accept it as a mere mistake or lapse of judgment. I needed to understand more. The journey that I took from then has been a fascinating one, to understand our magical, mysterious and temperamental brain, the control tower, cockpit, CPU and grand master of each of us. We can't learn to think smarter without investigating the master tool and Swiss army knife in our set of thinking tools.

Looking but not noticing

Please put on your inspector's hat and cape and join me on my investigation through the murky streets of our mysterious mind. Firstly, I'll present you with evidence to support my discovery that each one of us overlooks big and small things every day, and it isn't our fault. This is a finding that insurance companies will never acknowledge!

Over time computers have become faster and faster, but our dear old grey matter hasn't really progressed at the same lightening speed. It still has other winning attributes though, such as our ability to comprehend and produce complex emotions. (Having just read about the very first wedding ceremony that was conducted by a robot in Japan, I do marvel at what the future holds for artificial intelligence and us.)

Computers take in information in many ways — keyboard, mouse, wireless interface, touch screen, USB and a number of other input devices. In a way these are the computer's 'senses'. Everything that we know about the world around us has to originate with one of our five senses. We can only think about the things we can see, hear, feel, taste, touch and smell. There is also much talk of a sixth sense, but I'll have to leave that topic to those who know more about it than I do.

If our senses are our input devices, then the only way we can understand the world around us is to take in information through either seeing, hearing, tasting, touching or smelling something. We rely on our five senses for every type of decision that we come across, whether small or large. No book on decision making would be complete without discussing the role that our physical body plays in our decision making and problem solving.

Fast Fact

Our senses are an important part of decision making and problem solving because all our decisions must begin with some kind of sensory input.

Seeing the whole picture

Unfortunately each of our senses is somewhat limited in how it receives and transmits information. This can have serious implications for our decisions and, therefore, our actions.

If there were major mistakes in a movie, you would notice them, right?

Did you notice the 210 continuity errors in *Titanic* or the 44 errors (and counting) in *Iron Man 2*? Maybe you noticed the crew member with a white cowboy hat that appeared on the Black Pearl in *Pirates of the Caribbean*, along with 241 other mistakes that the continuity editors failed to pick up (according to www.moviemistakes.com)? No? I didn't either.

"Whenever you read a book or have a conversation, the experience causes physical changes in your brain. It's a little frightening to think that every time you walk away from an encounter, your brain has been altered, sometimes permanently."
— GEORGE JOHNSON

In my critical thinking training programme, I show participants a short video of about three minutes. During these three minutes they see an inspector questioning household staff in a murder investigation. Every time there is a close-up shot of the inspector's face, several pieces of the setting are changed, even the character playing the deceased changes. At the end of the video I ask what changes had happened. I am always rewarded with a sea of blank stares. No one ever notices that 21 changes occurred while they were watching.

We all suffer from what's known as change blindness. This occurs when we fail to notice large or small changes in a picture or scene. The change must usually coincide with some sort of visual disruption, such as the blink of an eye.

Now take a couple of seconds to read through the numbers below, noting which is the highest number. Then turn the page.

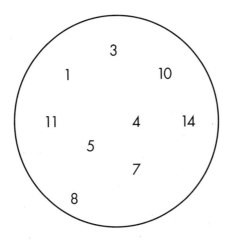

Now find the highest number again and *see* which number has been changed.

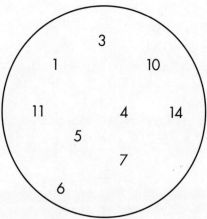

Did you have to flip back to the previous page to find the answers? Even though you had to look at each of the original digits to find the highest number, you may still have missed which digit had changed.

 Fast Fact

> Our limited short-term memory and attention span leads to us remembering surprisingly little of what we see.

These natural limitations have interesting consequences. Everyone only remembers a portion of what they see and, given the uniqueness of each of us, we are all likely to remember different aspects of the whole picture or conversation. Therefore we all interpret information from our environment differently. There is a very useful lesson in this: we try to never be 100 per cent confident in what we hear or see. In a disagreement, for example, different interpretations of the same subject usually crop up and should be allowed for. A smart thinker will always be asking: "What am I missing here?"

Finding your blind spot

Are you starting to see the bigger picture or are there still gaps in it for you? When it comes to seeing the bigger picture, our eyes deceive us. Let's do a bit of investigating now into the tricks that keep us all believing that what we see is real. We will discover that what we don't see is also real.

If you are reading this in a public place I suggest that you wait till you get home to try this next exercise. Hold the page really close to your face. Cover your right eye and focus your left eye on the X. Now slowly move the book away from you and notice what happens to the O.

| A | O | X |

Did it completely disappear from view? The O disappears but the A on the far left is still visible. If you move even further away the O reappears. Not only does the O disappear but in its place you see the nice smooth grey background. Weird, isn't it? What just happened?

You found your blind spot! On the retina of each of our eyes is a spot where the nerve must pass through. Here we have a physical blind spot where we can't see anything. Instead of seeing a blank spot, our brain and eyes collude to create a smooth viewing experience for us and, literally, fill in the blanks.

Which of your senses do you rely on most to gather information in everyday decision making and problem solving? If you didn't say eyes, and all your five senses are in good working condition, I bet eyes came in a close second. The limitations of our senses are a very real factor in determining the quality of our decision-making process.

Myth Buster

I have 20/20 vision so I can see everything that is in front of me, and seeing is believing!

Unfortunately, this can never be true, given that we all have a blind spot in our eyes that can't see anything. We don't notice it because our brain fills in the blanks with information that it can see.

Now, I think I know what you're thinking. What if someone's job relies on their ability to notice things? Maybe they are a doctor, radiologist, editor, auditor or someone who scans hand luggage for dangerous materials at the airport? Surely they would be much better at spotting things than the rest of us? After all, they would be looking for specific things such as symptoms of illness, signs of cancer, spelling mistakes, accounting anomalies, or a bomb.

"Chiie" is not the same as "Chile", even if no one notices

I had a chuckle the other day when I read in our local newspaper that the Chilean mint had minted a batch of coins that read "Chiie". Yes, the country's name was spelt incorrectly (an *i* replaced the *l*) and had gone undetected for two years. Could thousands of people have missed this little typo? Absolutely. What are you missing every day when you gather information, drive your car, review a new marketing campaign, or edit the press release that has to be written and approved in less than 30 minutes?

Let's have a look at one of those groups that is continuously coming under the spotlight. A radiologist has the very important job of spotting cancers and other diseases on x-ray film. At some point in our lives, any one of us may rely on a radiologist to diagnose a potentially life-threatening cancer. I find it worrying that the reported error rate for a radiologist hovers at 25 to 30 per cent, with 80 per cent of these errors from things that are actually visible on an x-ray but are overlooked.[3] Despite substantial improvements in technology and training, a human's ability to spot anomalies hasn't improved significantly.

 Aha! Moment

If you have ever failed to notice something really important and asked yourself; "How could I have missed that?" Don't be too hard on yourself. It happens to everyone. Even professionals who are trained to notice specific things get it wrong surprisingly often.

To be honest, knowing that other people also missed things that they were looking at directly didn't make me feel any better about ramming my beloved car into a pillar or forgetting that taking the baby for a walk meant that the baby actually had to come along with me. So my investigation continued until I finally discovered something that soothed my conscience.

"The brain is a wonderful organ. It starts working the moment you get up and does not stop until you get into the office."
— ROBERT FROST

Our brain is a poor shopper

Experts believe that the processing capacity of our brains is about 100 bits per second. I have no idea what that means either, but it all becomes clear when we consider how much information is actually presented to the brain by our five senses.

3   Shively, Christopher M., "Quality in Management Radiology", *Imaging Economics*, Nov 2003.

If I walk into a supermarket with only $10, I can buy a few goodies that total up to no more than that. If I have a hand basket, I should be able to fit them comfortably into it. Now imagine you are shopping at the mega mart with a cheque for a whopping $11,201,000 that you have to spend immediately. There's a catch, of course: you only have a hand basket to carry everything in. This is a metaphor for what our brains face every day. They are presented with millions of bits of information per second with only a hand basket to put them in. On top of that, while our brain does have a warehouse for extended storage, this warehouse can only be filled one shopping basket at a time. This means that our brain has to decide what to squeeze into its little basket to take back to the warehouse and what to leave behind on the shelves.

Our senses are responsible for generating all this information and stocking the mega mart shelves. Here's how much each one is thought to provide:

Eyes (vision): $10,000,000 worth of goodies

Ears (hearing): $100,000 worth of goodies

Skin (touch): $1,000,000 worth of goodies

Nose (smell): $100,000 worth of goodies

Mouth (taste): $1,000 worth of goodies

Is it any wonder, then, that we miss out on large chunks of information?

 Fast Fact

Our brain cannot physically process all the signals coming in from our five senses. Its shopping basket is too small.

Danger Zone

If two people have a different opinion on a certain subject, we usually assume that one person is right and the other is wrong. Given what you now know about our brain's limited ability to process lots of information, do you still think that disagreements are always clear-cut? Neither person may be wrong nor right.

Try This

Try to remember the last disagreement you had with a friend, partner or spouse. Write down the details of the argument from your point-of-view and theirs. Can you see how the same facts, images or situations can be interpreted differently by different people?

Sometimes we don't see or hear something that someone else has. They are not wrong but neither are we. If our brains can only process a limited amount of information, what happens to the rest of the information that doesn't fit into the hand basket? The rest is deleted, distorted or generalised. This helps our brains cope with massive amounts of incoming information.

Try This

Sometimes we give very clear instructions to people only to find later that they were totally misinterpreted. If you are working on something really important, it's worth asking them to repeat it back to you in their own words, to check if they have received it correctly.

But hang on, if we only use 10 per cent of our brains, surely we could just activate the remaining 90 per cent and process all incoming information? Problem solved!

Not so fast! Think about this: different parts of our brains are responsible for different thoughts, processes, functions or actions. If we used 100 per cent of our grey and white matter we would be doing everything that we are capable of doing all at once. We would probably fuse like a light bulb hit by a power surge. There is also no area of the brain that can be damaged without impairing our ability to function normally. We use 100 per cent of our brains, just not all at the same time.

 Myth Buster

> Everyone knows that we only use 10 per cent of our brain's full potential. If we can access the remaining 90 per cent that just sits there dozing, we would all be able to think smarter without too much effort.
>
> This is a very popular myth that has motivated millions of people to work harder at being smarter. It is a shame I have to tell you that there is absolutely no scientific evidence to support it. In fact, evidence shows that every part of our brain is used when called upon to perform its particular function.

At the end of my investigation, I feel better about having an imperfect processor that works slowly, misses out on important details and deceives me. After all, everyone has one!

Of course, finding the problem is not the same as finding the solution. What solution should we be looking for? How to patch up our blind spot, how to give our brain more bandwidth so that we can process more of the incoming information? Should radiologists, auditors and editors have Lasik surgery to improve their vision?

The solution to dealing with our physical limitations is not figuring out how to overcome them but learning how to work with them more effectively. Understanding that they exist and how they affect us is the first step in reducing their impact on our thinking process. We need to understand that when we process information, or think about things, the thoughts that we have are based on the information that our senses have gathered. This information must then be processed by our brains, which have limited processing power.

Does this mean that we aren't as smart as we think we are? How do we know how smart we are? What evidence do our senses gather that help us decide how much of the smarts we've been given? Is this evidence being processed by our brain correctly? I'll leave these questions for you to think about.

Let me close this chapter by giving you some ideas to help us all work with the effects of our physical senses and processing power on our ability to make great decisions.

Star Tips for making the most of your personal thinking tools

1. Understand our brain's physical limitations and how they affect us. This is the first step in reducing their impact on our thinking process.

2. Remember that everyone will interpret information differently. How we each see, hear, taste, feel and smell the world becomes our reality. It is our own unique interpretation, and this will be different for everybody.

3. Don't automatically assume that someone else is wrong because they didn't see or hear something that you did.

4. Look at a problem in as many different ways as possible, both literally and figuratively, to help you find big and small details that you may have missed.

5. Ask yourself constantly, "What am I missing here?"

6. Ask other people, "What am I missing here?" or "What would you do differently?"

7. Avoid always being 100 per cent confident in what you hear or see. Ours brains cannot take account of all the sensory input coming at them at once, so they delete, distort and generalise information to help them cope.

8. Ask others to repeat what is expected of them in their own words, after you have given them important instructions. This way you will know if they have understood 100 per cent of what you have said.

9. Take frequent breaks and remember not to make important decisions when you are tired or stressed. You may regret it later.

10. Take a mental break before finalising a project or making important decisions. You will return to it with a rested brain that can hopefully find some errors or blind spots that you hadn't noticed before.

HARNESSING EMOTIONS IN DECISION MAKING

"Human behaviour flows from three main sources: desire, emotion, and knowledge."

Plato

4

Emotions are vital in decision making

When I am faced with a really important decision I write down all the pros and cons, spend time researching possible outcomes, stress test these possible outcomes, and take time to understand the system in which the decision will occur, before I commit to a final course of action. Yeah right! If I made only one decision a quarter, I could go through this textbook process every time I had to decide between alternatives.

We are all faced with hundreds of decisions every single day. How many decisions did you make before you reached work this morning? Waking up when the alarm goes off, or not, is a decision. Choosing your clothes for the day, what to eat for breakfast, whether to run for the train or to accelerate through the amber light at the intersection. Many of us also face the dreaded decision: should I exercise this morning or not? If you happen to stop by a Starbucks on the way to work, you would have had to choose from a mindboggling 87,000 different types of beverages (according to their marketing material). This is all before 9 o'clock in the morning.

Just thinking about it makes me exhausted. On top of all this, our brain has limited processing capacity and gets tired quickly. How is it that we are able to sail through these daily decisions relatively easily and not have to spend an hour at Starbucks stress testing our coffee options? You already know the answer to this. How do *you* decide what to order from a menu or which frock or tie to pull from the closet? That's right. You ask yourself a simple question, "What do I *feel* like drinking," or "What do I *feel* like wearing?" We use feelings every day in making all sorts of decisions. It's true, feelings are an integral part of our decision-making process. These are the 'gut' feelings that we all experience, except they don't come from the gut at all. They are made in the part of our brain that creates emotions. Let's call this part our *emotional* brain. The neurological term for this is actually the 'limbic system', but 'emotional brain' may be easier to remember.

LOGICAL BRAIN

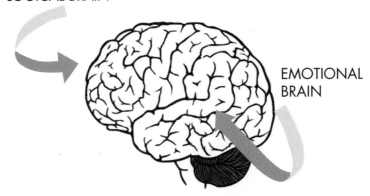

EMOTIONAL BRAIN

I have a host of books on my bookshelf covering the topic of critical thinking. Without fail they look at technical models, processes, analysis guidelines and flow charts, many of which I use myself. Often we use these models to remove the influence of emotions in our decision making. Decision Science is now proving that the missing ingredient in these models is the fact that they *don't* take account of emotions.

Emotions give us a starting point that guides us towards maximising our gain or pleasure, and avoiding or minimising loss or regret. Emotions are the very beginning of every decision we have, and will ever make.

Fast Fact

Feelings or emotions are mental shortcuts that speed up our ability to make decisions. They affect every stage of the decision-making process and, ultimately, help us make the best possible decision that we can, given our limited mental processing power.

Myth Buster

Emotions are fine in everyday decisions that aren't terribly important, but when it comes to really big decisions I should never let emotions get involved. So if I can just learn to block my emotions I'll make great decisions.

Not only is this impossible, but we wouldn't be able to make a single decision if our emotions were not available. If our emotional brain was damaged, we would struggle to decide between simple alternatives, such as whether to use a black or blue pen. When we did eventually decide, we would then be unsure of our decision and this cycle would continue.

Have you ever wondered how on earth your gut feelings are so strangely accurate?

Logic versus intuition

We can actively hold four to seven ideas in our working memory at any one time. This helps us compare different ideas or products logically. What happens when there are way too many choices for our thimble-sized working memory to remember and compare? When you are faced with 87,000 options at Starbucks, your logical brain is overwhelmed and is forced to check in with your emotional brain to get a helping hand, or thought.

> "Emotion is messy, contradictory... and true."
> — NIGELLA LAWSON

Aha! Moment

Our emotional brain can comprehend much more, much quicker than our logical brain. Often, when we are overwhelmed by facts, a lot of information is compacted into an intuition, or a gut feel. The inexplicable emotion, or hunch, that you feel is a messenger with a very important message. Trusting your gut isn't always the worst idea.

Fast Fact

Gut feelings aren't only useful in life-threatening situations. The part of our brain that generates these feelings is much faster than our logical brain. An emotional response or gut feeling will always be generated when we experience any kind of new information.

Find out how emotions slip into your decision making

Do you know how much emotions influence *your* decision making? Read through the following questions and jot down the first response that comes to mind. You may be tempted to change your initial response. If you do, write down both your first thought plus your revised response. For each of your initial responses, jot down which emotion was involved.

1. When you meet someone for the first time, how long does it take you to form an opinion of the person? If you later discovered that your initial opinion had been wrong, how long would it take you to change it?

   Response: _very quickly_

   Emotion: _____

2. You were offered a free gift with a purchase but you already have several of these and don't particularly need another one. Do you take it anyway or say "no thanks", to the surprise of the shop assistant?

   Response: _Take it anyway_

   Emotion: _____

3. Do you find yourself ordering the same thing over and over for lunch in a week when you are tired or particularly stressed at work?

   Response: _yes_

   Emotion: _____

4. You have to fire somebody who isn't performing particularly well at work. This person hasn't been there very long and you aren't particularly fond of the individual. How would you go about firing that person and how long would it take you? Conversely, if the person you had to fire was someone that *you* hired and had mentored, would your answer change?

Response: _a while_

Emotion: _____

5. You are a junior member of a team of designers and engineers working on the design of a new car for a major car manufacturer. Millions of dollars have been invested in this project. You notice a major fault in the braking system just days before it goes on sale. What would you do?

Response: _Get the issue fixed_

Emotion: _____

So how did you respond, and which emotions were involved? I bet that either minimising loss or regret, or maximising personal satisfaction or gain, was present in many of your initial responses. Strange, isn't it? If we look a little closer at some of them we will see that:

1. We are very quick to form an opinion of someone new. This is a mental shortcut. Here our emotional brain makes a decision purely on what we see, hear and already know about stereotypes, or the person we are meeting for the first time. Sometimes we make up our mind before we even meet the person! It usually takes us much longer to change our opinion, as we would have to accept that we were wrong, which leads to regret.

2. We don't often refuse a free gift because we might just regret it later.

3. Your brain (both the logical and emotional parts) gets tired. When it does, it points you in the direction of the last thing that made you feel good, or maximised your satisfaction.

4. You guessed it! It's much easier to fire someone that you haven't invested time and effort in. It's also much easier to fire someone that you didn't hire. Firing someone you hired and have mentored would mean admitting to a mistake, accepting a blow to your ego and experiencing regret.

5. See if you can find the emotions in this last decision yourself.

Our emotions aim to please

As I am writing, my housekeeper is roasting nuts downstairs in the kitchen. I am not hungry but I *am* desperate to get this chapter finished before my son gets home in a couple of hours. The thought of stopping, going downstairs and eating a couple of freshly roasted cashews is so overwhelming that I'm going to break my vow of 'not being distracted by anything' and nip down for a *proeseltjie* (pru-sil-kie), or little taste, as we say in my native language, Afrikaans.

This highlights another strange but powerful role of emotions in decision making. Not only do they attempt to maximise our pleasure and minimise our pain or regret, but they also try to do so in the shortest amount of time.

Let's have a look at an example of where emotions trump logic way more often than they should — the common weight loss diet. Have you ever been on a diet or fitness programme that failed? If so, how many times? Come on, be honest! Most of us go through at least one unsuccessful diet or fitness programme in our lifetime. Conventional wisdom points a finger at our lack of willpower or motivation, but it actually boils down to something far stronger than that — our hardwiring.

It's a lot easier to go on a diet at a time when we aren't faced with too many other challenges. What happens when we are upset, angry, stressed, tired or just feeling blue? Our emotional brain will search our memory banks for something that previously gave us a boost and helped us feel better instantly. Our emotions love to cheer us up. What could possibly make a dieter feel awesome for just a little while? You guessed it, chocolate cake, leftover pizza or a second glass of wine. These things offer instant rewards to maximise our happiness for the moment. This is exactly why the impulse to 'just have one cookie' is so strong. It's our brain telling our body to do what it has been programmed to do since the days of cavemen and cavewomen.

This is also why we can't resist a bargain or a 50 per cent off sale sign. We crave instant rewards and that little high that comes from knowing we got a great deal. This all changes when we get home and realise that the shocking pink clutch or Soccer World Cup tie doesn't match anything in our closet. What were we thinking?

Rogue emotions derail decision making

We've looked at the positive and important role that emotions play in every decision that we make. There's more to this story though. I know you have at least one example of where an emotion has gone beyond sending a subtle message to help your grey matter to make a decision.

 Try This

Can you think of a time when an emotion wreaked havoc on an important decision or hijacked your response to a situation?

Emotions are very fast. If you blink your eyes once you will know how fast a quarter of a second is. This is how long it takes your emotional brain to receive information and generate a response — an emotion. It takes the thinking side of our brain quite a while longer to catch up. This could be because our sensory input will have to pass through the emotional part of the brain before it hits the front where our logic processor is situated.

Think of the last time you cried in a movie or shouted at a driver for cutting you off. Was it logical to do these things? No. Did you do them anyway? Yes. If there had been more time to think about your response first, would you have responded differently?

> "I don't want to be at the mercy of my emotions. I want to use them, to enjoy them, and to dominate them."
> — Oscar Wilde

A recent local study showed that drivers with young children in their car are *more* likely to speed and switch lanes without signalling.[4] Can you imagine why? Emotions are certainly hijacking reason and logic here, way beyond sending subtle signals. Is this emotion trying to minimise pain or maximise satisfaction? Having spent many hours in cars with small children I would definitely say that it is trying to minimise the agony of having bored, hungry, tired, I-need-to-go-to-the-loo-now kids in the back of the car. This is the power of emotions in decision making.

The same newspaper ran a report from Indonesia where a man in charge of a shipping yard got mad at one of the dockworkers. In a fit of rage, he said some nasty things. His little outburst resulted in thousands of workers rioting, some being sent to hospital, and the boss himself getting seriously injured.[5] This was an entirely avoidable situation.

These emotions belong to our flight or fight response inherited from our wilderness-roaming ancestors. They serve us well when our lives are threatened and we need to make split second decisions. Sometimes, however, they can get a little bit confused about what exactly a life-threatening situation is.

---

4 Neo Chai Chin, "Driving Dangerously", *Today*. June 2009.

Danger Zone

Emotions that have the potential to hijack our ability to reason through a decision, are rogue emotions. They are out of line and out of order.

Write down a list of possible life-threatening situations that you might find yourself in. Depending on where you live, your list might be quite long. As a resident of Singapore, my list is quite short (with dangerous driving being at the top!)

---

5   Zul Otham. "Batam Dockworkers Torch Shipyard", *Today*. April 2010.

Did 'my boss telling me for the 10th time that I still haven't finished the report', or something like that, make it onto your list? Probably not. We aren't faced with nearly as many life-threatening situations as our ancestors were; yet this instinct remains very strong. That's okay because every now and again our survival still depends on it.

Myth Buster

Responding with an emotional outburst will let people know that I am very angry or upset, so they will take me seriously.

Picture this: if somebody responds to you by getting very angry and shouting, do you really listen to what they are saying?

An emotional outburst triggers the fight or flight response in the listener. He or she cannot hear your argument or message because they are too busy deciding how they will defend themselves against your outburst. They will have *less* respect for you because you can't control your emotional outbursts.

For every other situation that didn't find its way onto your life-or-death list, there is no reason to respond with an emotional outburst or let emotions rule your actions.

These rogue emotions need to be harnessed. Before we can harness emotions that lead us to make bad decisions, we need to know exactly what triggers our emotional responses and under what circumstances emotions overpower reason.

Fast Fact

We don't need to be able to control every emotion that creeps into our decision making, only rogue emotions that hijack our ability to think before we speak or decide.

Identifying rogue emotions

A rogue emotion is like a bull. If left alone in a meadow, the bull will munch the grass and mind its own business. If provoked, it gets nasty, single-minded and very destructive. What can tick a bull off faster than one can say "olè"? A waving red flag, of course.

Unless we know what our red flags are, we will always have a hard time identifying when our decisions are in danger of being hijacked by an emotion. Do you know exactly what ticks you off? Try this exercise to help you understand which situations trigger which emotions. Being able to anticipate very strong emotions will allow you to manage conversations far better, prevent outbursts, and remain clear-headed when it counts the most.

Keep a response diary that tracks your responses to various situations, like the one on the next page.

At the end of the week, group your responses into 'useful' and 'destructive'. A pattern will soon emerge where you can clearly see which situation triggers which response. Your emotional red flags will become very apparent.

My response diary

Day of the week	Monday / Tuesday / Wednesday / Thursday / Friday
What was said or done to me?	
How did it make me feel?	
How did I respond?	
Was my response useful or destructive?	
By the end of the week I think my red flags are:	

I spent some time keeping track of what made me hot-under-the-collar and I discovered some interesting things. My red flags appeared again and again, and I always responded in the same way to them. My two biggest red flags are *apathy in others* and when *people jump to conclusions*. If somebody says *no* to an idea or request before thinking it through or giving it a try — because it may involve some extra effort — I see red. I experience the physical symptoms of anger: increased adrenaline, faster heartbeat and warmth, and my tone of voice and body language become very hostile. The same happens when people jump to conclusions; I get defensive and lose interest in the conversation. As you can imagine, both my red flags have a very negative influence on my problem-solving ability, as my response diary clearly highlighted.

Fast Fact

Knowing what *your* emotional red flags are will allow you to be one step ahead of yourself and anticipate rogue emotional outbursts or destructive responses.

It's useful to know when the bull is going to charge, but wouldn't it be even better to get it to walk instead of gallop, or even to stay put in the meadow munching grass? It's not terribly useful just to recognise your emotional red flags unless you learn to *manage the raging bull*!

Tips for managing emotions

Don't have difficult conversations or make decisions when in a rush

If you are forced to make a decision or handle a difficult conversation in a rush, your logical brain can easily become overwhelmed and let your emotions take over.

Don't rush difficult conversations or decisions

There is no need to agonise over every decision, but it is very important to know which decisions can rely on instinct or gut feel and which decisions need quality thinking time.

Count to five before reacting emotionally and breathe deeply, always

You've heard this before but now you know why. This will give your logical brain time to catch up with your speedy emotions.

When making an important decision always ask what emotions are involved

What emotions could influence your choice? In what way would you be trying to minimise loss and maximise gain to yourself? How would everyone else involved be doing the same thing?

Talk to yourself and reflect on your actions every day

Professional sportspeople review their performance in detail. They watch recordings of themselves and their opponents, always studying how they can improve. Their earnings and sponsorship depend on it. We seldom do the same. Reviewing our responses, decisions and how others responded to us will improve our professional performance.

Get enough sleep

Every now and again, we may be expected to burn some midnight oil. This is fine once in a while. However, if we don't get enough deep sleep our brain's and body's ability to restore itself and retain information deteriorates rapidly. New parents fully understand how lack of sleep impairs their ability to remember, think critically and deal with unexpected situations. The rest of us may well sacrifice sleep in the hope of improving productivity. However, sleep is an essential ingredient in *determining* productivity.

Tools to manage emotions

Stepping back; from the basketball court to the boardroom

I'm not really a fan of basketball, but there is a basketball move that I think is absolutely brilliant. I've seen players do it many times and it always helps them get a shot at the hoop. I started sharing this in my programmes on emotional intelligence, and it is now helping many executives to reduce the impact of emotions on their decisions.

I call it the Step Back Skill. A basketball player will run straight at the opposing team. He gets so close to them that he rubs shoulders with those nearest; he looks forward and takes another step right towards the hoop. Of course, his opponents think that he will continue going forward, so they back off a bit. This allows him to take a mighty leap back into an empty space and shoot for the hoops.

In the same way, when faced with an important decision, we can get up close to our emotions and experience them fully. After all, they *are* going to happen with or without our permission. But once we have rubbed shoulders with them we need to take a big step back and ask ourselves exactly which emotion we are experiencing and why. When it is time to shoot for the hoop, we need to ask how our decision would change if we removed the emotion from the equation.

Minding the gap

There is not *nothing* between receiving information and responding. There is a gap. At the very least, this gap lasts for a quarter of a second. If we are aware of our emotional red flags, then we should be able to use this gap to catch an emotion before we express it. Over time, if we are consciously aware of this gap, it will get big enough to allow us to assess and filter a response *before* we say it. This doesn't take long. We would just need another quarter second.

MIND THE GAP

Someone who angers easily has a small gap and tends to become a product of their environment, unable to take charge of their own emotions and destiny.

If you have a small gap, try this: find a filler phrase that you can use, without having to think about it first. This will give you a couple of precious extra seconds before responding. An example could be:

Well, I can see why you think that.

Mmm, here's what I'm thinking.

Now that's an interesting/valid take on it.

That sure is one way of looking at it.

Can I take a mental step back here?

Design a filler phrase that feels authentic for you, and watch how it harnesses emotions, transforms interactions and widens your gap!

Star Tips for avoiding emotion-based decisions

1. Don't try to remove emotions from the decision making process. It can't be done.

2. Listen to your gut feel. It is an important part of how we process information. It supplements our logical brain's limited processing power.

3. Know that your emotional brain will always try to cheer you up and look for instant rewards. But these aren't always what's best for us in the long run.

4. Use a response diary to identify your emotional red flags.

5. Recognise what triggers rogue emotions. This will allow you to anticipate them and harness them before they land you in trouble.

6. Don't have conversations or make decisions when in a rush.

7. Get enough sleep. You will never be productive in the long run if you don't.

8. Count to five before reacting emotionally. This allows your logical brain to catch up with your emotional brain.

9. Develop your Step Back Skill to experience, understand and harness emotions in your decision making.

10. Develop a filler phrase that can prevent an emotional response and widen your input-response gap.

THE MENTAL BLOOPERS THAT WE ALL MAKE

"Nothing fails like success."

Arnold Toynbe
(historian)

5

I like nice cars. I have no idea how they work, nor do I want to know. I just know that expensive ones look gorgeous, go fast and are way out of my budget. Having no idea how a car works can be a problem. My very first car was not very nice to me. It broke down every time it rained heavily. Getting stuck on a highway in the pouring rain at 7 o'clock in the morning in Africa, alone with no idea how to fix your car, is definitely a problem. In my second year of car ownership I was stranded seven times. It was an expensive year. If I could have rolled up my sleeves, opened the bonnet and cast a beady eye over the engine to find the problem, perhaps my boss wouldn't have suggested that I use my first salary increase to buy a new car. Although I never learnt how to open a bonnet, I did eventually buy a new car.

Most car owners know a little something about how a car works. When it breaks down, it's helpful to know what the problem might be. If you do, mechanics can't take advantage of your ignorance and you won't be charged for a new part when the old one could simply be repaired.

Do you sometimes set out to solve a problem and end up making it worse? How about your decisions? Do they sometimes turn out in ways you didn't expect and you have no idea why? We all drive our own decision-making processes and use our mental engine to solve problems every day, but very few people understand what happens inside this grey box. So when it breaks down and we get outcomes that we weren't expecting, we don't really know how to fix the problem. If we could all be brain mechanics and learn to identify the sounds and symptoms of problems in our decision-making process, we would know how to identify and fix mental engine trouble. We could keep our engines working efficiently, smoothly and quickly, getting us from point A to point B faster and smarter than anyone else. What could be nicer than a smart, fast brain? Something everyone can afford to own.

Over the last 20 years, scientists have been opening up the bonnet that has kept our mental engine a mystery, and we are slowly learning about the inner workings of our brain. Although we are still a long way from compiling a comprehensive user manual, we can piece together something that looks a bit more like a troubleshooting guide.

A troubleshooting guide for your brain

In order to troubleshoot we have to look at our troubles. Let's start with a quick quiz to see what decision-making troubles you face.

Have you ever found yourself thinking or saying any of these things? If you have, put a tick next to it; if you haven't, put a cross.

❑ I've seen this before, so I know exactly what is going to happen.

❑ Well that's what everybody is saying, so it must be true.

❏ This is how I do it and it's always worked for me, so this is how you should do it too.

❏ It is on sale for 20 per cent less, so it must be a bargain.

❏ He is an expert, so I can trust him.

❏ I can't stop now; I've invested too much in this project. I'll definitely make the losses back. Just give me some time.

❏ We should do it this way because that's how it's always been done.

❏ I knew it all along. I could have told you that was going to happen.

❏ Well, you know what *they* say.:.

Of course, we all say or think some of these things, but sometimes it's hard to recall the details. For the rest of today or tomorrow, make a note every time you hear someone say or *you* say or think any of these things. If you ticked any of the above, try and remember the details and see how it fits in with any of the mental bloopers mentioned in this chapter.

 Fast Fact

Everyone suffers from mental mistakes or bloopers, but most of us are never aware of them until it's too late.

I can't seem to find agreement on how many thoughts our mind produces in a day. The reported figures run from 12,000 to 60,000 — a really broad range. As big as the difference between a 12 and a 60 horsepower engine! Many of our thoughts are subconscious, such as whether we are hot or cold, thoughts that tell our muscles how to move, and loads of other things that we really don't need to be aware of. Of course, other thoughts are really important and lead to critical decisions in our lives — who to marry, what jobs to accept, whether to trust someone or not, whether to tell the truth or not, and countless others.

What does our engine need to turn thoughts into great decisions? Just like any high performance engine, it needs top quality inputs. Good information from our senses, enough glucose and nourishment (it uses 20 per cent of the body's glucose supply) and loads of oxygen (20 per cent of our oxygen intake as well). Frequent rest and support from a healthy immune system will help keep it in tiptop shape. Unfortunately some inputs are not so welcome and, until recently, seemed unavoidable. These inputs are mental mistakes or bloopers that find their way into our thoughts surprisingly often.

Fast Fact

Over 150 mental bloopers have been studied and documented; way too many to discuss here.

A brain blooper, is a common mistake or error of judgment. We all make them, at some stage, when we process information. If we are to avoid them and their consequences, it's important to know how they affect our thinking. These mental mistakes are of particular interest to investors, casino managers, marketers, sales people, the management team at your local supermarket, and any other profession that makes money out of influencing the thoughts and, therefore, the decisions of others.

Why bother with brain bloopers?

- To understand that we make mistakes that we aren't even aware of.

- To recognise mistakes in the decision making of others which can affect us.

- To better predict how other people will respond to our decisions.

Troubleshooting tip 1: Don't take mental shortcuts

Shortcuts get us to where we want to go quicker. They save time, energy and sometimes, money. There's no harm in that really. A mental shortcut works in exactly the same way. Our brain uses more oxygen and energy (enough to power a 20 watt light bulb) than most of our other organs. However, the brain is very lazy, and it doesn't like to use energy 'willy nilly'. It would rather store it just in case it's needed later. Therefore, our brain develops shortcuts to help us deal with unfamiliar situations while at the same time conserving energy. These shortcuts are automated ways of thinking. This automation helps us get things done quicker.

 Fast Fact

Mental shortcuts help us adapt to new situations by looking for familiar patterns.

Imagine mastering the art of opening a can of pickles only to discover that you had to start from scratch again to learn how to open a bottle of ketchup! Once we can open one bottle, we can adapt that knowledge to open almost any bottle. In the same way, if we can drive a manual car, we can drive an automatic with little intervention. These are mental shortcuts. Here our brain looks for patterns, and groups what we know about opening jars or driving cars into general categories — *ways of opening jars* and *ways of driving cars*, among other things. These categories become general rules of thumb. These work so well for us that we use them as much as possible. There are times when taking shortcuts is not such a good idea though, as you will see in the other troubleshooting tips here.

Troubleshooting tip 2: Understand how easily available information shapes our opinions and decisions

What are your answers to the following?

1. Americans are...

2. Italians make the best...

3. Which causes more deaths globally; armed conflict, suicide or traffic accidents?

Now write down how confident you are that your answer is correct.

1.

2.

3.

Now write down what the source of your answer is.

1.

2.

3.

Are *all* Americans self-confident or good speakers? That's not possible and not true. Do Italians really make the best pizza? I've just returned from my second trip to Tuscany and I can assure you that this is one rumour that really needs to be put to rest. I do love Italian gelato and their coffee is fabulous, but good pizza is not guaranteed. Is your answer to the last question based on recent news reports? According to information from the World Heath Organisation, suicide causes more deaths every year than armed conflict globally, and either more or the same as road accidents in every region. Aren't we all rather confident in our opinions, most of the time? However, when we are asked to measure *exactly* how confident we are, we can start to doubt ourselves or question where our opinion comes from. Sometimes we even change our minds and become a little less sure of ourselves.

 Myth Buster

If someone tells me something, then I should assume that what they say is 100 per cent accurate. It would be highly offensive not to.

Not if done politely. Probe someone's facts a little with questions such as, "That's really interesting. Where can I get more information on it?" or 'That's fascinating. What's the source of your information?" This is not offensive at all, and an answer such as "Well, I heard it from my cousin who heard it from a waiter at the KFC who heard it from a client." might give you a clue that you need to research their facts before you make any important decisions based on them.

I recently received an e-mail from my son's school. In it was a warning that a lady had allegedly approached a nanny and the child in her care at a street corner. She had offered to give them a ride home. Fortunately the nanny was sensible and knew that taking a ride from a complete stranger was out of the question. The e-mail was sent to alert us and make sure we always knew where our children were and how they were getting home. Unfortunately, these events had, allegedly, happened around the corner from our home. A week later rumours were flying about two *abductions* that had happened just next door to us, and prospective homeowners were steering clear of the area.

Wow! Nobody knew the truth, and there were no results of an official investigation. Word-of-mouth has become such a powerful tool that it can shape opinions and change decisions in ways that seem illogical, with hindsight.

 Myth Buster

I am well-informed. I base my opinions on what I read, see on the news and hear from other people.

Did you ever play broken-down-telephone as a child, where a story is whispered into someone's ear and then gets retold several times over? (You may have called this Chinese Whispers.) The last person to hear the story then repeats it out load, often with hilarious consequences as it has usually been twisted and bent out of shape. People talk about what they see on the news or read or hear about. Stories get retold many times over, and facts get blurred or *enhanced*, sometimes through ignorance or for dramatic effect. It would be too time-consuming to check all the facts we hear and get the correct picture of our world for ourselves.

The *availability blooper* shows that our judgment is heavily influenced by how easily we can recall information.[6] If you know someone who was affected by an airplane accident, you might not fly for a very long time because it is unsafe to do so, in your experience or opinion. Yet flying remains the safest form of travel available. This is exactly what happened after the terrorist attacks of September 11, 2001. Both

---

6   This phenomenon was first reported by psychologists Amos Tversky and Daniel Kahneman.

holidaymakers and business people cancelled their flights and took to road travel. Unfortunately there were six times more deaths on the road in the four months that followed than in those four fatal flights that killed 256 people.[7] It was cheaper than ever and still far safer to fly than to drive, but thousands of people made decisions and put their families at risk based on faulty and emotionally charged logic. The less time we have to make a decision, the more heavily we rely on these mental shortcuts. This is also true if we have too many alternatives to choose from or if we receive conflicting information.

 Aha! Moment

When problem solving or making any kind of decision, my brain will use a last in, first out system to recall information and facts. It attaches greater significance to information that is easier to recall. This is why top-of-mind information always seems to be the most important.

Becoming aware that brain bloopers exist is the first step in reducing the effect they have on really important decisions. The second step to dealing with the availability blooper is to ask a few simple yet powerful questions:

- What/who is the source of my information?

- Where did my source get it from?

- Am I presuming anything?

- What are my presumptions based on?

- Am I only using the latest information that I have seen, heard or read?

---

7   Gigerenzer, Gerd. *Rationality for Mortals: How People Cope with Uncertainty* (Evolution and Cognition). Oxford: Oxford University Press, 2008.

Before we go on, I need to draw your attention to the meaning of the word *presume*. To *presume* is not the same as to *infer*. Inferring is a very important role that many people get paid handsomely for. To infer is to form an opinion based on the facts at hand and one's own personal experience or ideas. To presume is to guess based on little or no evidence.

Troubleshooting tip 3: Don't let framing (and fresh fruit) affect your decision-making processes

Imagine yourself walking through the doors of your local supermarket. What is the first section you walk into? I bet it's not shelves full of diapers or insecticide. Could it be fresh fruit and vegetables? How did I know? Because supermarkets are laid out the same everywhere, from the Tesco in Phuket, Thailand to Sainsburys in Southampton, England. But surely we don't really want to buy bananas and tomatoes and then carry on to pile cans of soft drink and boxes of washing powder on top of them later? We all know why chocolate bars and candy line the aisles at the checkout counters, but surely we should buy bulky stuff first and then move on to the delicate dragon fruit last? I'll leave you to think about this for a moment.

Once you have an answer for the riddle above, try solving this next one. Have a look at this sequence of numbers:

5 - 4 - 9 - 1 - 7 - 10 - 3 - 2

The numbers 6 And 8 have been omitted. Can you see where they belong and what the sequence is? This should be a breeze if you are good with numbers.

Thinking space:

Got it yet? Most people find this sequence tricky or just plain impossible. I'll give you a clue. It is the most common sequence that most of us work with every day.

If you are ready for the answer, read on. This problem is presented numerically, which makes you think in numbers. I mentioned that those good with numbers should find it a breeze. Very sneaky of me. In fact, these numbers are in *alphabetical* order, which is hard to see if you are in a numeric frame of mind. Very often a problem seems to stonewall us, and we simply can't find the solution no matter how many times we go over the facts or the problem. This is another mental blooper called *frame dependence*.[8] How a problem is presented or framed can influence our final decision as much as, or more than, the facts of the matter.

Fast Fact

'Framing' is a mental blooper that happens when how a problem is presented is as important in our final decision, or more, than the facts.

---

8 This phenomenon was also first reported by psychologists Amos Tversky and Daniel Kahneman (1986).

Very often the solution is not in getting more facts but changing the frame of mind with which we see the facts. Lateral thinkers and those trained in creative subjects purposefully change their frame or perspective on a problem to come up with better solutions, faster. There are several decision-making tools that help us avoid this trap, and we'll have a look at some in Chapters 8 and 9. Meanwhile, here are some tips to avoid the framing blooper.

Tips for tackling the framing blooper

- Acknowledge that there is always another frame of mind or perspective with which we can approach a problem. Our initial frame of mind may not be the only one or the best one.

- Sometimes we will be in an emotional frame of mind. If we are happy, excited or celebrating a victory, for example, we may not want to ask hard and cynical questions.

- In the same way, if everyone is excited about a project, it can be hard to draw attention to the negative aspects and ask what the potential pitfalls and losses could be.

- On the other hand, if we are optimistic or extrovert by nature, our approach or frame will tend to focus on the benefits and positive aspects of an issue.

- If we are pessimistic or cynical by nature, we will first explore the dangers and risks of a problem.

- Very often, it is hard for us to step out of our initial frame and take a holistic view of a problem. Changing the frame with which we view a problem is much like changing the channel on your TV. It must be done consciously, and we need to remember that one isn't more important than the other.

Did you work out why we are welcomed by fresh fruits and veggies at the supermarket when we really should be allowed to pack heavy and bulky items in our shopping cart before shopping for mangos and mushrooms?

Because they smell fresh and healthy, the colours perk us up, and each one of our senses receives a riot of information. Our stomach learns that we are surrounded by good, fresh food, and this makes us want some. It puts us in a good frame of mind and makes it easier to part with our hard-earned cash. Definitely not something that shoe polish or shampoo would do for us!

Do experts always make great decisions?

According to Wikipedia, "Experts have prolonged or intense experience through practice, and education, in a particular field. In specific fields, the definition of expert is well established by consensus, and therefore it is not necessary for an individual to have a professional or academic qualification for them to be accepted as an expert. In this respect, a shepherd with 50 years of experience tending flocks would be widely recognised as having complete expertise in the use and training of sheep dogs and the care of sheep."

We tend to think of experts as professionals such as doctors, lawyers or accountants, but we are all an expert at something. What does it take to be an expert then? 10,000 hours of specific practice? This is about 10 years if we spend four hours a day, 21 days a month refining a specific skill. Sometimes it is very hard to imagine what we are an expert at. Think of what you have been doing five days a week for the last 10 years. Some people are experts at parenting. Others are experts at their jobs, hobbies, selling or crafting.

Try This

What are you an expert at? What have you spent 10,000 hours refining over time. Is there anything you can do really well that you don't have to think too hard about, you just know how to do it?

Being an expert in any field has many advantages. Having loads of experience means that you have a mental databank of possible problems you may encounter as well as their solutions. You know what has and hasn't worked in the past. You can make decisions quicker than novices, and are able to understand and structure information faster and more easily. This leads to increased confidence and more effective problem solving.

Most English speaking adults are experts at English. It's true, we've spoken for more than 10,000 hours. (My husband says that *I've* spoken enough for two lifetimes.) So let's have a look at something that we all know, the English alphabet. Say it with me:

$$A - B - C - D - E - F - G - H - I - J - K - L - M - N - O -$$
$$P - Q - R - S - T - U - V - W - X - Y - Z$$

Now, cover the alphabet up with your hand and, without peeking, say it backwards just as quickly.

Did you find that challenging? Most people do.

Being an expert can have a downside too. Based on what you have just experienced, what do you think it could be? Mastering a skill or craft is hard work and a fantastic achievement. After some time, we usually reach a point at which we stop actively learning and as a result, stop broadening our knowledge base. Unfortunately, the challenges that we face don't stop evolving and getting more complex. When we continuously approach new problems with old, tried and tested techniques, there is a danger that the problems outgrow our solutions. When our old techniques fail us, we might have been caught in the expert trap.

I see it often in the public speaking industry. There are speakers with more than 20 years of experience who are very polished speakers but don't embrace new technology or update their content to connect with a younger, globally-savvy audience. They may be experts but it's not helping them stay relevant.

Tips to avoid the expert trap

Update: Continue looking for new ways to do what you do well.

Risk: Step out of your comfort zone and try a fresh approach.

Learn: Find out how other people, perhaps with less experience, are doing what you do. Can you learn from them?

Look: Stay on the lookout for clues that your approach might be outdated.

More troubleshooting tools to snoop out bloopers

Admitting that each of us can make mental bloopers is an important first step. After that, the quality of our decision making can be significantly boosted with some more simple steps.

Try these suggestions:

- Look for evidence that tests your ideas, not merely confirms them.

- When receiving negative feedback, avoid the natural tendency to dismiss it or find fault with it.

- Imagine that you disagree with your own project or decision. What fault could *you* find with it?

- It's also important to gather opposing opinions. Actively seek out at least two or three contrary opinions. Find two people who disagree with you *before* you finalise a decision. This is great free advice and could save you heartache later on.

Isn't it better to ask for opposing opinions before you finalise a project or decision than to get negative feedback afterwards, when it may be too late? Why do I recommend two or three opposing opinions? Well, it's easy to dismiss one for any number of reasons but when two or three people give you similar feedback, it's very hard to ignore.

These steps are surprisingly hard to take. But if you want to develop a smooth and efficient mental engine that can make the best possible decisions for you, you will need to take the necessary steps to avoid mental bloopers.

Star Tips for avoiding mental bloopers

1. Accept that we all make mental bloopers. This is the first step towards making better decisions.

2. Challenge your own opinions. Are they based on good information, guesses or on hearsay?

3. Infer, never presume.

4. Keep a lookout for the frame in which problems are presented.

5. Be aware that your mental frame of mind will affect your problem-solving approach.

6. Examine complicated problems through as many different frames as possible.

7. Celebrate being an expert at something, but watch for clues that your skills might be getting outdated.

8. Remember that challenges evolve in unpredictable ways. Your expertise must be continually updated to consistently meet new challenges.

9. Look for evidence that tests, and not just confirms, your thinking before you finalise any decision.

10. Gather at least two or three opposing opinions before finalising a decision.

COMFORT ZONE THINKING

"A wise man makes his own decisions; an ignorant man follows public opinion."

Chinese proverb

6

Your decision-making comfort zone

Here in Asia, 'thinking outside the box' is an enormously overused cliché. I'd guess it's overused in other parts of the world too. Someone, somewhere must have known exactly what and where our box is, but forgot to tell the rest of us. If you have ever found your box and managed to get outside of it, you stand to make a packet of money from your discovery. In my experience, the *box* is nothing more than a metaphor for uncreative thinking and narrow decision making. The good news is that there are very real reasons why we struggle to come up with ground-breaking solutions, make the same mistakes over and again, or find it hard to go against the status quo. This is not because we have our head in our box, but rather because we are creatures of comfort and habit. Our comfort zone plays an enormous role in the alternatives that we come up with and the decisions that we make.

Fast Fact

Comfort and habit are far greater influences on our ability to think creatively than our legendary box.

If all decisions in life were multiple-choice questions, almost every one of them would have these options:

- Do nothing
- Procrastinate
- Do what's always been done
- Ask someone else to do it for you
- Do something different

Let's face it, making important decisions is difficult. It's also harder to make great decisions when you have to decide on, and investigate, the alternatives yourself. Sometimes our problems loom so large that we hide from them and hope they will go away by themselves. Even easy decisions can be hard to make if you're in the wrong frame of mind. It's tempting to blame our *problems* for being difficult or impossible to solve, but before we can pass blame we need to understand how our comfort zone affects our problem-solving abilities. It may surprise you.

As we explore the options we usually have when faced with decisions, you might see how the first four could be the four sides of our mythical box.

How big is your comfort zone? Answer the following questions and decide how comfortable you really are.

- Do you ever go back to the same holiday spot two years in a row?

- Do you believe the adage: *if it aint broke, don't fix it*?

- How many times have you moved house in the last 10 years?

- How many times have you moved country as an adult?

- How long have you been working with the same firm?

- How many times have you bought the same brand of car?

If you only make big changes in your life when you are forced to, then you probably have a big comfort zone, like most of us. We are creatures of habit, and our comfort zone is carefully constructed over time through our trials and errors. Perhaps you return to the same holiday spot because you always have a peaceful time there. Why move house or country if you are perfectly happy where you are? What's the point wasting time improving something if it works fine the way it is? These are all sensible reasons for staying in our comfort zone.

In our comfort zone, we can work and live with no discomfort or risk. We only need to do enough to keep things the way they are. We stay in it as much as possible because stepping out is challenging, risky and frightening.

Danger Zone

Staying in your decision-making comfort zone is fine when it comes to picking a holiday spot. Not wanting to step out of your comfort zone when making tough decisions can lure you into accepting the default option of *doing nothing* and accepting the way things currently are, otherwise known as the status quo. Better options might never be explored.

Here are five reasons why we accept the status quo:

- Making decisions is difficult. Accepting the status quo and staying in our comfort zone is not.

- We may be faced with too many alternatives. This can be overwhelming.

- Remember that we make decision for one of two reasons; either to avoid loss or risk, or to gain something. Losing the status quo and risking an unknown gain are good reasons to do nothing.

- We may have already invested too much in the status quo. We have spent time, and maybe money, on previous decisions and it would be hard to change things now.

- The cost of gathering information on the alternatives could be high or time-consuming, and it is quicker and cheaper to go with what we already know, even if it isn't the best.

> "To do nothing is within the power of all men."
> — SAMUEL JOHNSON

Myth Buster

Once I have made a decision, I have to stick with it no matter what. Changing a past decision would be like admitting it was wrong.

Sometimes we go to great lengths to justify previous decisions. This protects our egos and reputation. This may even mean making a string of bad decisions to avoid admitting we were wrong in the very first one. In the short term this may seem like a sensible decision but the long-term consequences can be devastating.

My first novel has been sitting on my bookshelf, unpublished, for six years. The thought of having to find an agent or publisher, figure out how to submit it and then to face almost certain rejection, has always been too much for my ego to handle. As long as it's sitting on the bookshelf, my ego and I are happy. We think it's a little gem and we like the idea that nobody has criticised it. I would rather leave it unpublished because the risk of it being unloved by a publisher is more frightening to me than the gain of it actually being published.

The dangers of comfort zone thinking

Here are some of the consequences of letting our comfort zone lull us into regularly accepting the status quo.

- Supporting a failing project for longer than we should.

- Searching for fewer alternatives than we should.

- Keeping leaders, governments or employees in their positions for much longer than they should be.

- Accepting poor service because we don't want to complain or make a fuss.

- Accepting the default option, even when it isn't the best option, because investigating other options is too expensive or time consuming.

- Staying in relationships, jobs or living environments that may not be the best for us.

Fast Fact

Highly successful people regularly step out of their comfort zone. They know there can be no breakthroughs without some risk.

Great thinking happens outside of our comfort zone

How do we challenge the status quo and make it easier to create something new, make a difficult decision or go against the flow? Here is a buffet of ideas to get you uncomfortable with comfortable thinking.

To identify your comfort zone. Ask yourself:

- How have I done this before? What am I most comfortable with and what would make me uncomfortable?

- Is there a decision or choice that would make me feel very comfortable in the short term, and how tempted am I to take it?

- Is the status quo still the best option for me? How long has it been since I have re-evaluated it?

- Set specific goals for the decision or challenge. This will help you change focus from the options at hand to the required solution and work backwards from there. Ask yourself what are your ultimate objectives? Does the status quo suit those objectives now and in the future?

- If too many alternatives are making it difficult to decide and you are tempted to select the default option, could you find ways of reducing the number of alternatives before you reach a conclusion?

- If you have very few options and the status quo looks to be the best, have you checked out other alternatives you haven't yet considered?

- If the status quo didn't already exist as the default option, would you choose it?

- Is the status quo simply a handy option that can be chosen to avoid making tough decisions?

- Do you have a very strong commitment to the existing status quo that will prevent you from going against it?

Myth Buster

I would love to come up with great ideas and creative solutions that challenge the status quo, but I never seem to get any inspiration. I think you have to be born a creative person to have great ideas.

Think again! Great ideas are hard work and inspiration doesn't just happen. Creative people and expert problem solvers make a habit of constantly questioning the status quo.

"This 'telephone' has too many shortcomings to be seriously considered as a means of communication. The device is inherently of no value to us."
— WESTERN UNION INTERNAL MEMO, 1876

There could be absolutely no progress in this world if everybody accepted the status quo. Every invention has come about because someone wanted to do something better and was prepared to feel uncomfortable, take on some risk and step out of their comfort zone. Sometimes you not only have to challenge your own comfort zone but other people's as well.

Is procrastination your pressure cooker?

Don't look at my website. It's embarrassing. I need a new one and my company branding needs to be overhauled. I have known this for some time. I have had a focus group look at it and suggest what needs to be done, and I know what improvements I want to make. What do you think my excuse is for not having tackled it some months ago? Yup, time. Isn't that the excuse we usually use? But if a client called me up and asked for a proposal by tomorrow, I would burn the midnight oil and get it out. My website has the potential to bring in much more business than one proposal. It impacts my future income. I am probably *losing* business because prospective clients are turned off by my confusing and hard to navigate website.

My name is Tremaine and I am a procrastinator.

Danger Zone

Be careful of blaming a lack of time for not getting to tasks and decisions. Time is seldom the problem.

Fast Fact

Not prioritising tasks or decisions properly is a major cause of procrastination. Procrastination is one side of our uncreative box.

Perfect procrastination takes practice

If you are not a procrastinator, skip the next section. If you are, read it now. Don't put it off till later.

Do any of these scenarios sound familiar?

- You do the quick and easy things first to get them out of the way. Then have no time left to tackle the big jobs.

- Even though you are given sufficient time to complete a project, you only seem to get to it just before the deadline.

- Some days you just don't feel like doing certain jobs, so you put them off.

- You complete a piece of work only when you feel so guilty about not having done it yet that it's hard to focus on anything else.

- You miss deadlines constantly.

 Danger Zone

Do you ever think, "*strange, I was really busy all day but I didn't achieve anything significant*"? An inability to prioritise decisions and commit to a daily agenda is a poor work habit. It can lead to low productivity despite being busy during the day and tired at the end of it.

Try This

Write down all the things that you have been meaning to do but never get around to. Grade them as a) nice to have, b) not important for the moment and c) important. Now, ask yourself what's stopping you from doing the really important things?

Why do we procrastinate?

Sometimes doing nothing is not an option. Action must be taken but we don't want to do so for a variety of different reasons. Procrastinators...

- do the fun stuff first.

- don't always have a proper task management system so seldom know exactly which tasks are due and by when. It's only when they get reminded, or see an imminent deadline that they take action and rush the project through.

- find challenging the status quo so daunting that they prefer to do nothing, for as long as possible.

- usually find it hard to make a decision and commit to it. Decisions seem so final.

- wait until they have the *time* to do important things.

- try to manage time instead of managing the tasks that fill it.

If you are a procrastinator, I'm sure you can think of your own reasons for procrastinating certain projects.

Aha! Moment

There really is no such thing as time management. Unless you are the God of Time you can't control time. What you can control are the tasks that fill up your time.

Tips to kick the procrastination habit

Have a clear daily, weekly and monthly plan. Spend at least 30 minutes once a month, 15 minutes once a week and 10 minutes every day on task scheduling. Use a diary, blackberry, iPhone, iPad, notepad, whiteboard, calendar — like Google Calendar or Microsoft Outlook calendar — to note your deadlines and what you need to achieve for the month, week and day. Remember to break big tasks down into bite-sized daily activities. Here are some more tips:

- Prioritise activities for each day and make sure that you start with your top priority. This way, if you do nothing else for the day, at least the top job can be ticked off.

- Allow yourself the fun stuff but only after the top priority is taken care of.

- Enjoy the feeling of getting something important done every day. Then recall the stress of chasing last minute deadlines and rushing through tasks that you could have done weeks ago. Now decide which you prefer!

- If you are putting off a hard-to-make decision, remember that it will have to be made at some point. The sooner you make it, the sooner the pressure of it looming will be relieved.

Myth Buster

I work best under pressure. So it makes sense for me to put projects or decisions off for as long as possible.

This may backfire! Leaving things till the last minute is always risky. Something unexpected may crop up and force us to abandon our plans and best intentions. Working and making decisions under pressure seldom leads to the best possible outcomes, especially if there are complications. Thoroughly thinking things through takes time and is really difficult to do under pressure.

Conventional wisdom isn't always wise

Sometimes we decide not to decide because we don't have to, maybe because our boss or someone else has decided for us. They may know better than we do. This is conventional wisdom, something that everyone just knows. As I get older (remembering that I'm not that old, yet) I have come to realise that conventional wisdom is a lot less *whiz* and a lot more well, *dumb*, than I had always thought. Let's check the meaning of conventional wisdom to make sure that we are both thinking about the same thing before we talk about its influence on our decision making.

"The conventional view serves to protect us from the painful job of thinking."
— *JOHN KENNETH GALBRAITH*

"Conventional wisdom is a term used to describe ideas or explanations that are generally accepted as true by the public or by experts in a field. The term implies that the ideas or explanations are unexamined and, hence, may be re-evaluated upon further examination or as events unfold." — Wikipedia

Fast Fact

Ideas that are unexamined, but are accepted as true by experts or the public, are considered to be conventional wisdom.

It's this last bit that's important for our decision making. Decision makers often use ideas that are taken for granted, or generally accepted, as inputs in their decision making. Can you think of some examples of conventional wisdom that we do not usually question?

Here are some that I come across regularly:

- A vegetarian diet will help you lose weight.

- Only women get breast cancer.

- Mom or Dad always knows best.

- Open plan offices are more efficient and increase productivity.

- The boss should never be questioned.

Here are some old ones that have been proven false:

- Safe as houses! (property is *always* a safe investment)

- Employees could never work from home because they'd be unproductive.

- If you are the boss, you need to be tough and task-orientated to make sure that employees respect you and deliver the goods.

- Women have no place in the workplace; they should be at home with the children.

- The earth is flat.

Conventional wisdom leads to all sorts of decision-making evils. When conventional thinking is an input in decision making, it is seldom challenged because it's widely accepted. Rooting out *any* given facts in a problem and challenging the assumptions underlying them may change the dynamics of the problem considerably.

 Aha! Moment

Questioning popular thinking is uncomfortable and requires one to make unpopular choices. When making critical decisions, popularity is not more important than having sound judgment.

Like challenging the status quo, questioning conventional wisdom is not a skill that comes easily or naturally to most of us. If leaders and visionaries do not question socially accepted assumptions, we would never advance. Airplanes would never have been built, women would never be on equal footing to men, planets outside of our solar system would never have been discovered, and life as we know it would be very different to the way it is today.

What are the assumptions that you use in your daily decision making? Perhaps sometimes you assume that you know how someone feels without asking them? I always assumed that my son wouldn't eat mushrooms, especially shiitake mushrooms, because three-year-olds don't eat mushrooms! It turns out that it's his favourite food, at the moment anyway. What does mummy really know? Some people assume that it's ok to download music illegally because so many other people do it. I used to assume that if someone drives a fancy car they were rich... until I moved to the East. In Asia, having a fancy car is the ultimate status symbol. Many people live in small apartments, take out a loan and live a frugal lifestyle just to be able to afford a luxury sedan.

Right now, as I complete this manuscript, the Gulf of Mexico is experiencing a massive oil disaster, with up to nine million litres of oil seeping into the ocean every day from a shattered oil well. This has led our leaders to question the widely held belief that any future economic growth is heavily reliant on oil. Thirty years ago, the idea that a country could thrive without its own steady supply of oil was inconceivable.

> *"Oil is the lifeblood of America's economy." It is 'the basis and the moving power of modern industrial society and is therefore indispensable'.*
> *— United States Department of Energy, 1974*

This may result in a huge paradigm shift that overturns conventional wisdom, if not now then at some point in the future.

Five ways to challenge conventional wisdom

Here are some questions that you can ask yourself and your team members to help highlight any conventional thinking in your decision making.

- Check all the pieces of information that you use when making a decision. Which ideas are fact-based and which are widely held beliefs?

- Are these beliefs based on someone's past experience or are they merely what everybody believes to be true at the moment?

- If any of these beliefs turned out to be false or different, how would that effect the decision?

- Is your solution truly the best one or is it simply the easiest, quickest, cheapest or the default option?

> *"The man with a new idea is a crank — until the idea succeeds."*
> *— MARK TWAIN*

Danger Zone

If you are ever in a position where you need to question authority, remember to question the issue at hand only, not the person's right to authority.

Try This

Pick up your pen and write your name with the hand that you don't usually use to write with. For most people this is their left hand. Notice how it feels. You have probably been writing for many years and are quite comfortable doing it with your dominant hand. It may feel challenging, awkward, slow or just plain weird.

The feeling you get when writing with your non-dominant hand is often how it feels when you are stepping out of your comfort zone and challenging your brain to explore new ways of thinking. Of course, it gets easier to do with practice. It is only when we step out of our familiar and comfortable way of doing things that we get inspired, produce our best ideas, and deliver our best work. It might not always feel comfortable but, over time, the rewards far outweigh the effort.

Star Tips for avoiding comfort zone thinking

1. Remember that comfort and habit are far greater influences on our ability to think creatively than our legendary box.

2. Accept some discomfort. Nothing significant can be achieved without it. Making decisions is difficult, but accepting the status quo and staying in our comfort zone is not.

3. Step out of your comfort zone by challenging old ways of thinking about and doing things. This will put you on the path to success.

4. Find ways of reducing the number of alternatives when too many are making it difficult to decide and tempting you to select the default option.

5. Make a habit of constantly questioning the status quo.

6. Check if you're selecting the status quo because it is more comfortable than making a tough decision.

7. Generate more creative solutions by asking yourself and your team, "How can we do this differently?"

8. Control the tasks that fill up your time. This is more realistic than trying to manage time.

9. Root out any given facts in a problem and challenge the assumptions underlying them. This may change the dynamics and conclusions of the problem.

10. Question popular thinking. It may be uncomfortable and require you to make unpopular decisions, but when making critical decisions sound judgment is more important than popularity.

CREATIVITY PRODUCES BETTER SOLUTIONS AND BREAKTHROUGHS

"If new ideas are expected then people will make an effort to have new ideas."

Edward De Bono

7

The great creativity myth

A slither of sunshine slipped through the gap in the blinds. But it wasn't the cool morning sun that woke Tae from her disturbed sleep. It was a bolt of mental lightening that hit her thoughts and blasted clarity into every nook of her brain. She sat upright, still confused. After a momentary silence, the pieces fell into place, undisturbed in her mind. She beamed. Could it be true? She had just figured out the cure for cancer. Would anyone believe that a first year student could have such a revelation? She would have to wait and see.

This extract would be a good start to a science fiction novel; probably a very short novel. But would anyone believe that a new student could wake up one morning with the answer to one of the most complex riddles of our time? Surely not. Yet there is always a hope that creative solutions will just dawn on us. That we'll wake up one morning and have the blueprint of the next big idea, or have found a way to solve our most pressing problems. Some people wait a lifetime for creative inspiration to come *to* them.

 Fast Fact

It is tempting to believe that great ideas just arrive, out of nowhere and when least expected. The truth is that all great ideas and creative solutions are manufactured over time.

Creativity is like a roaring campfire. A campfire is a complicated thing. You can't just throw down a pile of logs and command them to burn. Dry logs must be positioned in a certain way to allow for ventilation. A spark is needed to ignite a flame and, hopefully, set fire to the perfectly positioned pile of wood. My campfires always need a little fanning to get them burning brightly and more logs to keep them going till the marshmallows are roasted.

Throughout this chapter I'll give you some ideas on how to build your creative campfire by creating the right environment for idea generation. We'll also explore lots of different ways of finding that essential creative spark when working on projects, on your own or in a team.

Try This

In Chapter 6, we already explored some of the sparks that can ignite creative thought in problem solving and decision making. Can you remember what they are?

In case you can't remember, let me remind you. They are a) recognising when you have slipped into comfort zone thinking, b) challenging the status quo, and c) questioning conventional wisdom.

When creativity produces better solutions

Uncreative solutions are much like a pile of logs on the ground — something unremarkable that we can walk straight past without taking note of. I googled 'uncreative solutions' and got a message that read, "Did you mean: *creative solutions*?" followed by a link to accounting software. Uncreative solutions are far more common than creative ones but I guess they are not as newsworthy. Uncreative solutions make the world go round, but creative ones make it better, or at least more interesting. Can you walk past a roaring fire and not take note of it? I can't.

Here are some signs to help you identify when conventional solutions are no longer good enough and it's time to light that creative campfire:

- When the problem constantly recurs.

- When previous solutions stop working.

- When previous solutions make the problem worse.

- When previous solutions cause problems elsewhere.

- When you accept that there is no solution.

- When you settle for less or drop your standards, over time.

- When the current solution uses up more and more resources.

- When it is hard to get buy-in to your solution from all stakeholders.

- When average results aren't good enough.

- When you are bored with doing the same old thing.

Create an environment for growing creative ideas

A fire needs air to burn but it can't burn on air alone; it needs gas, wood, old telephone directories, report cards, letters from ex-lovers, or something. Take your pick, as long as you have something to fuel the fire. Creative ideas don't appear out of thin air either; they also need fuel. What can fuel the fire of creativity? Sometimes creative twigs will suffice and other times we need big creative logs. Logs and twigs take time to grow and so does creative thought. Here are some things you can do to nurture your seeds of creativity:

Get enough fuel for creative thought

Know your subject well. Tae may well discover a cure for cancer but probably only after she has researched her subject thoroughly, enough to have mastered it.

Know how the problem has been solved in the past

We don't like to hear it, but our problems are seldom unique. Nowadays we have extraordinary access to information and should be able to discover what has and hasn't worked in the past. This can save us time, resources and disappointment.

Get up to date

What is the latest best practice in this particular area? What do other people know that you don't? Again, we can learn from other people's experiences as well as our own.

Check out someone else's back yard

Have other industries or groups had similar problems? How did they solve or approach them?

'Z' marks the spot for creative ideas

Whether you need to grow a creative solution the size of an acorn or something more ambitious like an oak tree, your ideas will need some time to germinate in your mind. Frequent, short 'mental breaks' from projects and good quality sleep are essential for peak mental performance and idea generation.

> *"Some sort of incubation period, in which a person leaves an idea for a while, is crucial to creativity. During the incubation period, sleep may help the brain process a problem." — Mark Jung-Beeman, a psychologist at Northwestern University, USA*

Danger Zone

If you feel that you have explored many options but the solution is still not clear, hammering away at the problem will cause stress and frustration. Ideas don't grow well in this environment.

Myth Buster

When I have a difficult problem to solve, I can't afford to get hours and hours of sleep. I need to stay awake and keep working at the problem for as long as possible.

Contrary to popular belief, getting more deep sleep will enhance your problem-solving abilities, making it easier to come up with better solutions.

Fast Fact

According to research at Harvard University, if a break from a problem includes sleep, we are 33 per cent more likely to come up with a more creative solution than before, even though we are totally unaware of it.[9]

If you are lucky enough to work for Google, Cisco Systems or Procter and Gamble, you don't have to wait till you get into your own bed at home for some creative zzz's to help you solve a problem. They are among a handful of companies that have installed egg-like recliners with lids that

9   Berlin, Leslie. "We'll Fill This Space, but First a Nap", *The New York Times.* 28 September 2008.

block out noise and light, called *EnergyPods*. Employees are invited to take naps at work. It's no coincidence that these companies lead the race for creative innovation. Where do I sign up?

Brainwaves

Even in a dark, cozy pod surrounded by the sounds of flowing water, or whatever is piped through the speakers, I would struggle to fall asleep during the day. There is just too much going on from 8 am to 6 pm to block it all out for some shut-eye, even if I am tired.

 Try This

Write down what you were doing the last time you had a great idea or solved a problem in an original way?

Fast Fact

Our brains work at several different brainwave frequencies. Each is responsible for different types of activities.

Beta brainwaves are thought to have the fastest frequency and are generated mostly by the left side of our brain. It's no surprise then that they are responsible for logical and critical thought. As we get older, we have more beta brainwaves to help us cope with our everyday challenges. Beta is best for writing a logical exam, giving a speech, talking to the boss or anything else that makes us nervous or hyped up. Too much beta and we get stressed. Beta is action and output orientated. It's not going to produce a *eureka* moment for you. Your last great idea probably did not happen at your computer after 10 hours of hacking away at a problem, nor did it happen while having an argument with your spouse or being quizzed by your boss. It most likely happened while you were relaxing on a Sunday, out on a walk, or about to fall asleep — when you experienced slower brainwaves.

Fast Fact

Alpha brainwaves are produced when your body and mind are relaxed. Both the logical left and creative right sides of your brain can produce them. Thoughts are clear and calm. This is when we are able to make new mental connections and produce creative solutions.

This is also the brainwave with which we learn best. A glass of wine will get you surfing your alpha brainwaves, for sure, and so will meditation or slipping into those few moments when you are between being awake and falling asleep. Since most of us can't sip a chardonnay, meditate or fall asleep at the office, how can we generate alpha brainwaves to help us think of creative solutions? Here are some suggestions:

- Breathe deeply for several seconds with your eyes closed.

- Take the stairs and grab a cup of coffee away from the hubbub of the office.

- Keep photos of your last holiday on your desk and allow yourself to slip back into it with a little daydream. No one has to know.

- Listen to relaxing music on your iPod for a couple of minutes.

 Myth Buster

If I work harder, for longer hours and don't stop working on a problem until I have solved it, I will come up with better and more creative solutions than anyone else.

You may come up with more solutions but they will probably not be better. When your mind is stressed out or tired, it will struggle to generate great ideas.

 Fast Fact

Relaxed minds in a creative environment manufacture the best ideas.

Many solutions make for creative problem solving

Any diehard camper will tell you that there is more than one way to build a campfire. Sometimes you are stuck with nothing but soggy twigs and wet matches or cow dung. That's right, cow dung! In Outer Mongolia, my husband and I managed to make a campfire with nothing but cow dung. Apart from billowing smoke, it heated our dinner and our *ger* (Mongolian tent) very nicely for the whole night. Very eco friendly, I think.

 Fast Fact

Problem solving takes time and energy, so we tend to focus on coming up with only one solution.

 Danger Zone

Chasing only one, or your best solution, can lead down two dangerous paths.

Path 1: The one solution we choose doesn't work as planned and we have no plan B.

Path 2: We might decide too early on which is the best option to pursue and so cut ourselves off from exploring other, potentially valuable, alternatives.

When trying to solve a problem creatively, set yourself a goal of creating multiple viable solutions. This way you'll never be left wondering 'what if' and you will always have a plan B.

Better brainstorming for breakthroughs

Remind yourself now of how you go about leading a brainstorming session, or brainstorm on your own.

According to the originator of traditional brainstorming, Alex Osborn, there are four basic steps:

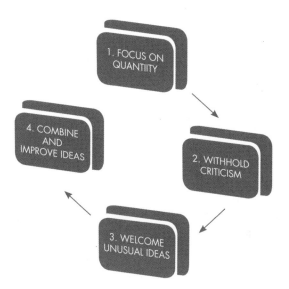

Using this traditional model of brainstorming; a problem is presented and everyone offers ideas on how to fix it. No one is allowed to judge or comment. Ideas are then combined and blended together. What happens next is up to the group. Some teams chose the best solution by majority vote, others discuss pros and cons and then let management make the final decision, and other people prefer to hammer it out till there is consensus. Don't forget the ever-popular anonymous vote.

The trouble with traditional brainstorming

Let's look at some of the shortfalls of traditional brainstorming:

- It's hard to tell if everyone has a good grasp of the problem.

- Volume and not quality of ideas is encouraged, which wastes mental energy.

- More vocal team members could drown out quieter members.

- In bigger groups, team members have to wait their turn to share their ideas, and sometimes those ideas get lost in the process.

- Very strong ideas get diluted down.

- Not being allowed to criticise and wanting to blend all the 'best' ideas tends to create compromised solutions.

- Nobody is responsible for coming up with an awesome solution and so free-riding is encouraged.

- Personal investment in the process can be low and rewards, if any, go to the group.

How do you feel about brainstorming? What problems have you encountered?

 Danger Zone

In its traditional form, brainstorming converges different ideas into compromised solutions. Breakthroughs aren't always guaranteed. Research supports this theory and has not found evidence that it effectively increases the quality of ideas generated.

Fast Fact

Brainstorming remains so popular because it is simple to do with groups of any size, and it can also be a great way of building team moral and motivating people.

On the other hand, if someone has ever demanded that you be creative on the spot, you will know how hard it is to do. This is often what is required of us in a brainstorming session. You may feel intimidated and anxious instead of motivated.

Intelligent brainstorming for breakthroughs

You have already read about how being tired and stressed affects our creative spark. To get the best out of a brainstorming session and from yourself, first invite participants into a creative frame of mind. Here are some ideas on how to improve on traditional brainstorming for breakthrough results.

Step 1: Prepare for the storm

It's often the case that we are invited to a brainstorming session well in advance and we know what the topic will be. As it's a brainstorming session, there is really no need to prepare beforehand. But imagine if we did? Asking each participant to think of, or investigate, their own best suggestion before coming to the session will vastly improve the quality of the ideas presented. It will also mean that nobody can eat the free pizza without offering a good idea in return. Each participant should share their own idea *before* the free flow of ideas begins, so no idea or person is drowned out.

Step 2: Warm up first

If you are looking for creative solutions, you can encourage your team to be in a creative frame of mind with a few exercises first.

- Improvisation: Display unusual or interesting items or photos and let each person pick one and suggest a creative use for it.

- Seeing the bigger picture: Sometimes team members get very bogged down in details and can't see the bigger picture or associate with big picture ideas. Try this exercise: take any of the items or ideas from the first exercise and 'chunk up on it' by asking yourself a chain of "what is the point of that?" questions, even if it is only based on conjecture. So a toothbrush would be: a tool to clean teeth; which helps to prevent cavities; which keeps teeth from rotting; this saves on dentist bills; which increases the profits of medical aid companies; which means that the bonuses for medical aid staff can be higher; and enable them to get their kids better birthday presents; which means that their children will get spoilt! And so on. Remember that this is meant to be a fun warm up and introduction to creative association. Keep it light and unstructured.

- Disruptive thinking: Prepare a list of products, services or practices that the company or group already offers. Ask participants how they would improve upon it if they had a generous budget. Alternatively, ask individuals to identify a piece of conventional wisdom that is used in the office, city, country, society etc, and then how it could be challenged.

 Try This

Depending on the nature of the problem and the group dynamics, you may like to try a number of different exercises to overcome different thinking obstacles and create a fertile environment to nurture creativity.

Step 3: Think up a storm

Now the group is ready to get down to the business of brainstorming. Here are some tips to extract maximum value and creativity from the group.

- Keep the group as small as possible so that everyone is able to offer ideas and opinions.

- Put everyone on the same page: Assume nothing. Ask for ideas about what caused the problem or led to the need to brainstorm. This will set the scene and make sure that everybody knows exactly what he or she is there to do. Write up different suggestions and notice how many you receive. Clarify and correct wayward ideas and faulty thinking. Note any ideas that are new and sensible.

- Provoke: Look for loose associations that can contribute lateral thoughts. Naming a new trendy shoe? How about exploring the names of hip or upcoming neighbourhoods in your target market. An energy drink? How about popular trends in action movies? My dad is an undertaker who is forever looking to improve the quality and range of services that he offers. He visits biker clubs and extreme sports groups along with medical associations and frail care centres to gather information on how to improve his offerings and best meet the needs of his clients in unique ways.

- Challenge conventional wisdom and comfort zone thinking: Flip back to the questions on page 99 that challenge comfort zone thinking.

- Play card games: Ask for ideas and solutions, which would ordinarily be spoken, to be written on cards instead, anonymously. Group the cards into similar themes.

Fast Fact

There are many examples of provocative questions leading to breakthroughs. Google questioned the need to charge for products and services. Wikipedia questioned the need to hire dedicated professional researchers and writers to write an encyclopaedia. Crocs asked why we couldn't wrap our feet in brightly coloured plastic. Twitter questioned the need to write long e-mails to stay in touch or use traditional advertising to promote a product.

Now, remember that brainstorming is a process to generate ideas that lead to solutions. It's not meant to generate the final solution. For that you need a more structured and analytical process. This may sound like a lot less fun than tossing ideas around and snacking on pretzels, but it doesn't have to be.

Disney's problem-solving process

Walt Disney was born with a wonderful imagination and a talent for drawing. This didn't make him an immediate runaway success though. It took many years, risks, a bankruptcy and lots of hard work, for him to build his magical kingdom and his legacy. Remembered as the creator of Mickey Mouse, he was also an entrepreneur and later, the man who ruled an empire generating US$100 million a year. It's no surprise then that he fused imagination and solid planning in his decision-making strategies. I'd like to share one of them with you that will help you transform the ideas from your brainstorming sessions into actionable strategies.

There are three distinct stages to his process, and each phase should be carried out in a different space or room, if possible (this is the way Walt Disney would prefer it), and there should be a time lapse between each one.

Stage 1: The Dreamer

This first stage is the brainstorming session, as previously described. Remember to plant creative seeds before the session by asking everyone to prepare. Set time parameters for each stage and try to stick to them. Honour participants' time by not letting the session drag on or go overtime. Play dumb and ask crazy questions like "what if?" and "why not?"

Stage 2: The Realist

This is the planning phase, in which team members should be disciplined and output orientated. For all the viable options selected in Stage 1, plan how each would be achieved, what resources would be required, and within what timeframes. This gives a good overview of which ideas are possible and fit in with your bigger picture and available resources. It also helps you get clear on exactly what the potential outcomes are.

Stage 3: The Critic

Over time, Disney learnt that even his most imaginative ideas would have to live and work in the real world. He learnt to become an avid critic of his own work. Idea-generation and group-planning sessions often fall flat at this point because nobody relishes openly criticising someone else's idea — especially if it's your buddy's best idea. The beauty of this process is that everybody is required to offer constructive criticism and nothing else during this phase. This changes the group dynamics and pressures on individuals. If your team is not comfortable offering opinions or highlighting potential pitfalls, it could be easier to lead the discussion with open questions such as:

- How, what, where, when and why can this fail?

- How will this impact other areas of the business (or life, if it is a personal project)?

- What are our competitors doing?

- Has something similar been tried before?

- How accurate is our information?

- What assumptions are we using in our planning and calculations?

Scenario testing should also be done in Stage 3. Ideas get chosen because they have potential, everyone knows this. The downside is often ignored because it is uncomfortable, very subjective and rather depressing to explore when a new idea is still very fragile.

Many projects that fail during a recession or a changing business cycle do so because the project team doesn't explore the question, 'What is the worst thing that could happen?' A worst-case scenario may seem very unlikely when the going is good, but things can turn when you least expect it. By preparing for both failure and success we can go into new ventures with our eyes wide open. There is no harm in being prepared for both the best and worst that can happen.

You should now have lots of ideas for kindling your creativity. One of the most important ideas is knowing that being creative doesn't rely on having some special inbuilt creative gene. Creativity is a skill that is built through conscious effort and deliberate practice. By following the steps in this chapter, you'll be well on your way to discovering your creative self.

I know this was a rather lengthy chapter. Creativity in decision making is so important that it needs to be thoroughly explored. I could never expect even the most creative of souls to remember and practise everything we've just chatted about. So how about doing a quick scan of the chapter, or even just the Star Tips at the end, and pull out some ideas that really speak to you, things that you will try and use from here on? Then note them down in the thinking space provided on the next page. This will give you an easy reference guide for the next time you need to light your creative campfire in a hurry.

Thinking space:

Star Tips for creating breakthrough solutions

1. Identify when conventional solutions are no longer good enough and a creative one is called for.

2. Foster a creative environment that embraces questioning and research.

3. Rest often and take breaks from working on a solution.

4. Try techniques to generate alpha brainwaves. This is when you'll have your most creative ideas.

5. Generate multiple solutions to one problem.

6. Break away from traditional brainstorming.

7. Encourage your team to contribute good quality ideas when brainstorming.

8. Ensure that everyone prepares for a brainstorming session.

9. Allow everyone an opportunity to share their ideas before the free flow of ideas begins.

10. Play with Disney's problem-solving process to transform ideas into solutions.

VISUAL TOOLS FOR PROBLEM SOLVING

*"Today's problems come
from yesterday's solutions."*

Peter Senge

The problem with traditional problem solving

Let's start off with a slightly offbeat exercise. Have a look at the picture and answer this question: What caused the driver to park his car in the swimming pool?

Whatever your answer is, ask yourself, "why?" and continue asking *why* for each iteration. Here's a real example of one of these exercises. Eight to ten volunteer *problem solvers* are lined up and asked to solve the problem using linear problem solving.

Respondent 1: The driver was intoxicated.

Me, "Why?"

Respondent 2: He had been out at a party.

Why?

Respondent 3: It was his farewell party.

Why?

He had resigned.

Why?

His boss was mean.

Why?

The boss's mother didn't love him as a child.

Why?

She was too busy with his three other siblings.

And so on…

Conclusion: The driver drove his car into the pool because his boss wasn't loved as a child.

Hey? I'm sure you're wondering what the purpose of this perfectly daft exercise is! When put into perspective, however, it teaches us a very powerful lesson about the limitations of linear problem solving. You have most likely been faced with a problem that seemed a little opaque initially. How did you tackle it? Most of us have learnt that the best way to tackle complexity is to break it down, to simplify it by asking why, what, where, when, who or how? And to keep plugging away at the problem till we uncover the cause of the cause. Then, with a pat on the back, we can declare the problem solved.

Myth Buster

Getting to the root of the problem means finding the cause of the cause.

This is traditional, or linear, problem solving at its best. It works well for simple problems but does more harm than good when applied to tricky or complex scenarios.

What problem-solving methods are you familiar with? Cause and effect analysis, tree diagrams, 5 whys, flow charts, USP analysis, force field analysis, SWOT and scenario analysis, to name a few. Some of these are great for quick fixes and show results in the short run while others are better with more complex problems and generating longer-term solutions. However, there are also times when traditional problem solving simply isn't enough.

Fast Fact

Generally, when traditional methods are applied to a complex problem, they start with breaking it into its parts in order to analyse and understand what caused the problem in the first place.

In fact, the word *analysis* is the opposite of *synthesis*; it means '*to break or dissolve anything complex into simple elements or its constituent parts*'. Analysis in problem solving is largely a linear exercise where x causes y, that is, something (x) results in something else (y). This makes us look for one-way, direct relationships. This approach is fine for simple linear problems but you wouldn't be eight chapters into a book on problem solving if all your problems were simple and linear!

Here is an example of a seemingly simple problem: once or twice a year, there is an outbreak of seasonal flu. Nothing too complicated. Loads of people fall ill, stay away from work for a couple of days and return when they recover. That's all fine. However, some people return to work too soon, or refuse to go on sick leave and spread the flu virus to their colleagues, which vastly increases absenteeism. What would your linear solution be? To make sick leave compulsory for a certain number of days or as prescribed on the person's medical (sick leave) certificate? This is only one possible solution. Can you think of any others?

Jot down your ideas here:

Do you suspect that this is actually *not* a simple linear problem? If we were to apply the simple fix of *mandatory sick leave*, related problems are sure to sprout in other areas. Why are some people returning to work before they are well enough to do so or not taking sick leave at all?

Here are some of my ideas:

- Taking time away from work may reflect poorly on the person and count against them later.

- Work piles up when on sick leave or away and it is hard to catch up.

- Something important may be happening at work and there is no one suitable to cover for the absentee.

- For some people, especially in expensive countries like Hong Kong, staying at home in small, crowded apartments is not conducive to recovery. Therefore, many people would rather go to work despite still being ill.

- For anyone who gets paid for hours worked, a loss of income may not be acceptable.

Can you see how a quick fix of *making sick leave mandatory* won't address any of these problems? Instead, it will make many of them worse, reinforce the initial problem and cause more absenteeism. Most of the organisational, social and technical problems that we face today cannot be solved using a linear problem-solving process.

Problem solving in the 21st century and beyond

We live in an interconnected world. Take a look out of the window. Everything, everywhere is connected to something else. These connections could be of mutual interest or dependency. Our world forms part of the solar system that is part of the galaxy. Our bodies, companies, government and country, buses, trains, people, plants, the weather and even Uncle Bob all form part of a system. Our problems do too.

Fast Fact

Just as everything in our world is connected to something else, tricky problems are too.

As I write this chapter, I have been reading about the new 'superbug', NDM-1, that has hit the shores of the UK from India. It seems to be resistant to every known antibiotic and poses quite a threat to our ability to eliminate, or at least control, infectious diseases. Initial news reports fear that it could be one of the deadliest pandemics of our time. Scary isn't it?

What caused its virulence? I am not a medical expert and will leave the technical reasons to those who are, but it seems that the widespread use of antibiotics over the last couple of decades has created bugs that are resistant to the very things that are meant to kill them. Every doctor that prescribed antibiotics (i.e. a linear solution) when there wasn't a 100 per cent need for them has contributed to this outcome. Of course, it's pointless to cry over spilt milk (or medicine). How this problem is addressed remains to be seen. The entire system within which it was caused and now flourishes in, will have to change. It will need a thorough and systemic solution. Hopefully though, your problems aren't on such a grand scale.

Let's take a look at how to tell when linear solutions will do more harm than good. In Chapter 7, we discussed how to spot the need for creative solutions rather than conventional ones. The criteria for identifying tricky or complex problems is similar:

- When there are lots of different ideas on exactly what the problem is.

- When there are lots of different ideas on exactly how to solve the problem.

- When brainstorming doesn't narrow solutions down but widens the field of possible answers resulting in confusion, frustration and even conflict.

- When previous solutions have unintended and unforeseen consequences on the problem.

- When previous solutions create unintended and unforeseen consequences in other areas.

- When the problem constantly recurs or solutions only fix the problem for a short while.

- When too much information is available to fit into an existing problem-solving model.

- When not enough information is available to understand the problem fully.

- When decision makers are not confident in their final decision.

- When decision makers feel as if they are plugging the holes of a watering can with toothpicks.

One of the best ways to investigate and solve complex or tricky problems is through a .system's approach that respects and models the interconnectedness of all things, from dealing with health and interpersonal issues all the way through to issues of government policy and technical or IT problems.[10] I was first introduced to a system's approach when I studied how to build large scale, complex databases and information management systems at university. I thought it was neat then but it really blew me away when I started using it as an investigative and problem-solving tool in areas such as coaching and organisational change management.

10 Senge, Peter. *The Fifth Discipline: The Art & Practice of the Learning Organization,* New York: Doubleday Publishing Group, 1994.

Let's use this example to explore what makes interconnectedness so powerful. If a ceramic vase is shattered, it can be repaired with some patience and glue, but it will never look the same again. The cracks will show where tiny bits of the vase have been lost forever. Unless modern art swings in the direction of traumatised vases, it will only be fit for the trash. The vase will never be whole again. Remember the definition of analysis? Once we have analysed our problem and attempt to put the pieces back together again, we sometimes end up with a piece of promising modern art rather than a solution. Often the deconstruction of a problem is destructive. It's often so destructive that when we attempt to put the parts back together, it's like gluing a broken vase. The pieces will fit and stick with glue, but the tiny fragments that fill in the cracks and smooth the surface will be lost, and the vase (or the problem) will never resemble its former state of wholeness.

Complex problems result from all the individual components acting together to produce a certain outcome. For example: one could study hydrogen and oxygen individually forever and never stumble upon water. It's only when you put them together that water results. Water is the *emergent* property that occurs when combining hydrogen and oxygen. If you then separate the hydrogen from the oxygen, you will no longer have water but rather two very different gases. By separating out the pieces of a problem to study them individually, you lose sight of their emergent properties or the heart of the problem.

Fast Fact

The things that make up a problem need to interact for the problem to occur. This interaction causes characteristics that cannot generally be seen in the individual parts of the problem.

Myth Buster

Every problem-solving approach must start by breaking the problem up into little bits so that we can understand it better and generate the best possible solution.

You'll be missing something if you do this! When we dissect our problem to simplify it, we strip its parts of their interconnectedness, making it impossible to understand the whole and appreciate or predict the result of the system at work. The whole really is greater than the parts.

A visual problem-solving toolkit

I like cars, but not cooking. So it's no surprise then that I am very familiar with the flopped cake. Squishy, mushy, or chip-your-teeth hard, lopsided creations have often emerged from my oven over the years. They have also been my apprenticeship in working with living systems. My mom, of course, can look at one of my culinary embarrassments and quip, "Oh just use less baking soda next time" or, "Your oven was too hot again, honey". How does she know these things when no two flops ever look the same? Because she understands the system in which a cake is created.

A cake is a closed system and a great example of a tricky problem. The ingredients, preparation method and environment all contribute equally to the final outcome. If any one of them is not exactly right, the whole system breaks down, along with the ability to attract friends over for tea. If a cake flops, one can't easily pinpoint the exact cause of the problem merely by looking at the result or breaking it up to analyse it.

If breaking a complex problem into little bits is a bad idea, what should we be doing to fix tricky problems and bake better cakes?

Here is a five-step plan for using a 360° visual problem-solving model:

Step 1: Get specific

Often there is uncertainty or disagreement on exactly what the problem is — who it affects, how long it has been going on, how far or how deep it goes. We take for granted that everyone is 'on the same page' and understands all the issues as well as we do. Other times we assume that we have all the facts and aren't missing anything. A great start is to define the current problem or challenge *not* in terms of possible solutions but rather ensuring that everybody is crystal clear on what the *problem* is.

Step 2: Get visual

A good way to make sure that everybody understands the problem and parameters is to make them visual. When complex issues are represented as diagrams, attention is moved from the debate to the diagram. This makes it easier when there are a lot of different opinions or strong personalities. It also clears up confusion because everyone can *see* what everyone else is *thinking*. It doesn't have to be fancy; a drawing on a napkin can be just as effective as a masterpiece on an electronic whiteboard. You will also find that everyone remembers the facts a lot better, as images improve our ability to remember details and retain information. Subtle differences in viewpoints or understandings, which could have resulted in problems later on, will become very clear.

Step 3: Get creative

Your drawing will need to show all the players and elements that interact to create the problem. This can include people, processes and things. It should also include people, processes or things that form part of other systems that interact with your problem. Define the boundaries of your system, and identify any unknown areas. For some people this phase is really challenging, but for those who love organising and making things clear and simple, this is a fantastic and creative exercise. There is the risk that these folks can get carried away and over-model the system into something that looks like a bowl of spaghetti dotted with meatballs. I am particularly gifted at creating meatball and spaghetti problem diagrams, and I always end up having to simplify them sooner or later! So, remember to stay focused on the problem at hand.

Step 4: Get thinking

Playtime is over. This is where the real business of problem solving begins. You'll need a thinking cap; fellow problem solvers and refreshments are also nice. This is where you define how all the elements in your problem relate to and react with one another.

For instance, the model below illustrates the two elements that interact in our absenteeism example from page 139, whereby 'flu season increases absenteeism' and 'absenteeism decreases productivity'.

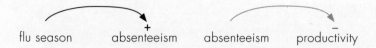

flu season   absenteeism   absenteeism   productivity

You can also define behaviours and the effect that behaviours have on other parts of the system. For example, the pressure to meet deadlines decreases employees' willingness to take sick leave. Remember to include time delays that create imbalances in the system over time. If absenteeism is frowned upon, it will create an unhappy, overworked workforce in the medium to long term. Time delays help to identify pressure points that could cause blockages or 'explosions' later.

Step 5: Get going

Think of a spreadsheet with lots of complicated calculations in it. If the calculations produce the wrong or a nonsensical result, the only way to fix it is to scour the formulas and numbers in the spreadsheet to see where the problem lies. It could be an unwanted zero, a space, or a plus or minus sign in the wrong place that throws everything out. You can't try and fix the *solution*; you have to examine the system that produced it. This is why it is so important to create a visual model to help everyone understand how the problem was caused in the first place. It is worth checking your model or drawing and making sure that, if it worked as agreed, it will produce the results that you expect. This is called evolving your diagram.

Now that everyone is clear on the problem, its causes and consequences; it is finally time to look for the solution. You will find this process goes much more quickly with a visual model than without.

As with a spreadsheet, we are looking for the place where the smallest tweak will change the outcome of the system and fix the problem. This is the leverage point. If the leverage point is not obvious, you must brainstorm for possible alternatives. Now, because you have spent some time designing a model of your problem, you can plug each of the different solutions into it and see how it affects the other players, and then consider what changes you would expect to occur and where.

A visual problem-solving shortcut

Over time I have developed a shortcut to help problem solvers remember all the elements they need to think about when modelling their problem. Let's call it the 'Gâteau model' in honour of my baking boos-boos.

Even if you are not in a position to draw a spaghetti diagram of your problem, this analogy will make sure that you think about all the things that could possibly impact the problem you are working on. It looks at everything needed to create and enjoy a cake, such as a baker or bakers, ingredients, an oven, layers of sponge cake, icing sugar, candles, and hungry mouths to feed. When you examine your issue or problem, identify the following elements in it. These are the things that interact to cause it:

- Baker/s: The people essential in making the system work. If we use the example of sick employees returning to work before they are better, then the *bakers* would be the sick employees, their bosses and colleagues.

- Ingredients: These represent the things that interact within your system. A good place to put the company leave policy and standard operating procedures for when someone is off ill, such as who checks their mail and responds to their clients etc.

- Oven: Here we have a very apt analogy for the environment in which a problem is baked. Are sick employees faced with a hostile, judgmental or competitive environment or a supportive, collaborative team? There may be many different views on the environment within which the problem has occurred. All views are important and should be considered in turn. It will soon become clear which one is most likely to be the prevailing one.

- Layers of sponge cake: Is your problem a couple of layers deep? Sometimes the symptoms we can see are really only the tip of the iceberg and there may be a lot more going on than what meets the eye. Could employees be coming back to work too soon for reasons that are not obvious? You may need to dig a little bit and speak to a few people to find out more. Perhaps there is some kind of social reward for returning to work as soon as possible?

- Icing sugar: Maybe your problem doesn't have too many layers. Instead it could be draped with icing sugar, giving it a smooth sugar coating over time. If it has taken some time for the problem to come to light or to be addressed, what has been keeping it off the radar screen? Have line managers been encouraging ill staff to return to work as soon as possible to avoid having extra work on *their* desks? The icing sugar may even be something as simple as the status quo that never gets questioned.

- Candles: Candles make a birthday cake special — at least until one's 21st birthday, after which they become a fire hazard. The flaming candles represent the emotions that are always present in any kind of problem and in the decision-making exercise used to solve it. What are the emotions that could be contributing to your problem? Self-interest, discrimination, feelings of entitlement or something else? What emotions are involved in the problem-solving process? Remember that emotions will always help us prevent loss of some kind or maximise a gain. Perhaps the human resource department feels the need to defend their policies (prevent loss) or line managers are very frustrated that the extra workload falls on them and they can never take sick leave themselves.

- Someone to eat the cake: There would be no purpose in baking a cake if nobody ate it. In the problem-solving context, those who are ultimately, and sometimes only remotely, affected by the problem would fall into this category. In our example, we could include customers who receive poor client service from a reduced workforce and inadequate sick leave policies. Maybe members of other departments or regions are also affected?

Voilà, that's it!

Try it for yourself. For the next time you need to solve a complex problem, I have included a diagram to remind you of all the players that interact in creating, or baking, a problem. This should help you find that all-important leverage point that could change the outcome of your system and, hopefully, solve your problem.

BAKER

INGREDIENTS

OVEN

CANDLES

ICING

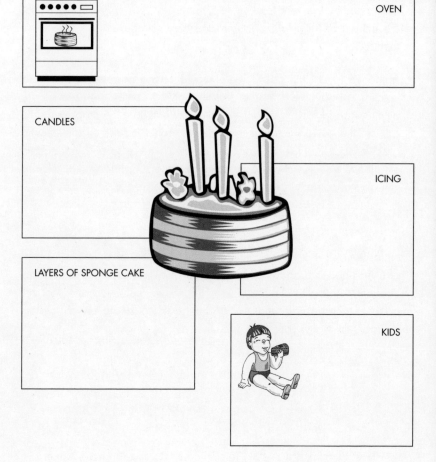

LAYERS OF SPONGE CAKE

KIDS

A note on getting started

Looking for new solutions to problems usually starts with a blank sheet or screen. Don't get caught up in how the problem or solution is depicted in the beginning. It doesn't matter if you start from the inside out, the outside in, the top down or bottom up, or any combination in between. Just start at the point that is top of mind to you.

Star Tips for using visual problem-solving tools

1. Decide if you are working with a simple or complex problem. Using a system's approach for a simple problem is pointless.

2. Avoid simplifying complex problems by breaking them up into little bits. Many important characteristics may be lost when you do.

3. Define your problem, not in terms of possible solutions, but rather ensuring that everybody is crystal clear on what the *problem* is.

4. Make your problem visual by drawing a diagram of it. This will highlight differences in viewpoints and understandings.

5. Diffuse disagreements or heated debates by focusing on elements within your diagram and not individuals.

6. Model interactions and time delays in your system.

7. Remember to define the boundaries of your problem and not to overmodel it.

8. Use your diagram to find the leverage point in your system. This is where your solution will come from.

9. Plug different possible solutions into your system to see how each one will work.

10. Use the Gâteau model to help you remember and investigate all the elements that should be considered when tackling tricky problems.

PRACTICAL PROBLEM SOLVING FOR TEAMS

"No problem can withstand the assault of sustained thinking."

Voltaire

The advantage of many minds

Ubuntu is the heartbeat of a multicultural South Africa. It describes how each person is one thread woven into the multicoloured fabric of society and can't flourish in isolation. It speaks of the interconnectedness between individuals as the essence of being human. If the fabric were unravelled, all the individual threads would stand alone, each one guarding a tiny fragment of the fabric's pattern.

Whether one is an introvert or extrovert, very few people can thrive in absolute isolation. There are many reasons why we like the comfort of being part of a team or group either socially or at work. Here are some:

- Being considered socially desirable is great for our self-image.

- Community spirit is emotionally supportive.

- We like to feel part of something that we can readily identify with.

- Groups help us define who we are and what we stand for.

Teams have also become the heartbeat of most organisations today. When it comes to decision making, there are clear benefits of groups thinking together. Most of these benefits come from the diversity of people.

Of course, if things go wrong, it's also handy to be able to spread the blame around!

 Fast Fact

Diversity of education, background, experience, specialisation, ability, perspective and opinion lead to very information-rich decision making and accelerated learning.

In his bestseller, *The Wisdom of Crowds*, James Surowiecki explains how a group of independent thinkers can collectively make very smart decisions. For a group to be wise and fully utilise their collective wisdom, there needs to be healthy diversity of opinions — opinions that are not influenced by the opinions around them, but by independent thought. There must also be some way to channel these independent thoughts to arrive at one outcome. The stock market ticks some of these boxes. Lots of analysts, drawing on specialist knowledge in various areas, research information on companies and form their own opinions on these companies' shares. The trading system is the funnel that aggregates all their ideas. Every now and again, things go wrong, markets tumble and crash, or spike and climb up into a bubble.

When independent thinkers are influenced by each other and their decisions start to look very similar, the group of individuals is no longer a wise crowd but a herd with collective behaviour and decision-making processes. On a much smaller scale, the teams that we work in are also perpetually tempted by the lure of falling into comfortable and easy patterns of thinking. Yes, comfort zone thinking happens to groups just as easily as it does to individuals, and sometimes it's even easier.

 Myth Buster

Companies prefer to use project teams rather than individuals, because teams always make better decisions.

Not always! An effective group decision-making process can yield extraordinary results but, like brainstorming, if it is not managed correctly you can end up with safe, mediocre compromises crafted to maintain the status quo or support ideals or agendas.

The disadvantage of many minds

In 1999 an incredible match took place. An unparalleled contest that pitted one man's smarts against the rest of the world's, literally. Gary Kasperov challenged the rest of the world to a chess match. They accepted and battled it out for four months. 75 countries united against Kasperov. At the outset it seemed a little crazy for one person to hope to beat the collective wisdom of over 50,000 minds, including grandmasters and veterans. Was it genius or madness? Time would tell. About half-way through, his competitors started showing signs of poor co-ordination, arguing, turf wars, profanity and all sorts of dynamics that took their energy away from the actual game and into interpersonal dynamics. Kasperov won.

Groupthink

Social psychologist Irving Janis first introduced the idea of groupthink. He used it to explain why otherwise rational people can make irrational or poor decisions when grouped together.

> *"Groupthink occurs when a group makes faulty decisions because group pressures lead to a deterioration of mental efficiency, reality testing and moral judgment."*
> — *Irving Janis*

Sounds a bit harsh doesn't it? Team-based decision making is a bastion of modern business not terribly different from how our forefathers used to hunt or gather in packs. But history and evidence bears out that something changes in our thinking patterns when we enter into the comfort of a group or the shadow of a cause.

Try This

Think back over the history of your country or religion. There were probably times when a group acted irrationally, with hindsight. Perhaps under the influence of propaganda or a powerful leader, individuals made decisions that they would not have made acting alone.

I hate to admit it, but sometimes, working in a team can be a real pain. Decision making is slow and discussions can go round in circles. We are expected to offer 'constructive' criticism yet have to tip-toe around sensitivities when we do. On the other hand, if my ideas go against the majority view, I'm vulnerable to questioning and probing and being overruled anyway. Sound familiar?

Even though diversity is what helps groups make great decisions, groups whose members have similar training, backgrounds or perspectives work much smoother than diverse teams. In hierarchical groups, positions are established and respected, and balance is maintained between members. Not upsetting this balance can sometimes be more important than airing individual views.

Aha! Moment

The closer members are in background and outlook, the more likely it is that groupthink can emerge organically.

Lack of diversity doesn't mean that groupthink is inevitable though. Strong, mature teams are also best able to debate topics and question each other without upsetting the group's dynamic.

Symptoms of groupthink

Fortunately there are some signs to look out for when you suspect groupthink has crept into your team's decision-making process[11]:

- A belief in the group's cause that may not be questioned. This contributes to members themselves not questioning their own actions.

- Unquestionable faith in the team's ability to produce outcomes. This is an important motivator in sports teams.

- Loyalty to the group and its ideas are encouraged. Membership is exclusive and those outside of it are labelled as different or not good enough.

- A not-made-here attitude that emerges when ideas that challenge the group are dismissed without being checked out first.

- The assumption that silence from members means consent.

Fast Fact

Groupthink is a mode of thinking. It changes the way information is received and processed by a group.

Consequences of groupthink

Symptoms of groupthink are usually harder to identify than the consequences. When a team's performance starts to deteriorate, it's worth keeping an eye out for these behaviours that result from thinking in groupthink mode.

Assumptions run free

If I assume I'm the only one who doesn't understand the problem or proposed solution, I'm certainly not going to speak up. I risk sounding slow or stupid in front of everyone. It's easy to assume that everyone else understands what

11 Adapted from: Janis, Irving, L., *Victims of Groupthink*. Texas: Houghton Mifflin Harcourt, 1972.

is being discussed. Ideas can go unchallenged and important questions can be tucked away under the blanket of assumption.

Alternatives and options are not as extensively examined

Groupthink raises the level of confidence in the decision-making ability of the team — especially following one or more successful projects. This reduces the incentive for members to question current modes of thinking or ways of approaching projects.

The past is never dug up

Past failures are always uncomfortable to dissect and examine, but the past is a great teacher if partnered with objectivity. When digging up the past leads to finger pointing and blame throwing, group harmony suffers. Such introspection is often avoided despite the very valuable lessons it holds.

Mental mistakes are supersized

If individuals suffer from mental mistakes, groups suffer even more so.

Plan Bs are for the B Team, not us

Backup plans can be forgotten or swept aside because of a group's belief in their ability to get it right the first time.

Role of the team leader

Team leaders are chosen for many different reasons. Perhaps they have the best technical knowledge or training, the most experience or the best relationship with the client concerned. Sometimes the team leader has the best team-management skills. Sometimes they are chosen because they are the boss. Whatever the reason, as the *leader*, their opinion weighs heavily in the decision-making process. Team leaders who need to get the best possible thinking out of their team may want to keep a beady eye on how much they allow their opinion to sway the group's thinking.

Danger Zone

Be wary of assuming that team leaders are chosen because they have the best technical knowledge and so should use it to influence the project as much as possible. This approach may work well with junior or inexperienced teams but may 'de-motivate' more experienced staff. The leader's role is not to guide the team towards a predefined outcome but to ensure rigorous debate and maintain a healthy group dynamic whilst contributing as a team member.

Turning groupthink into team think

Team thinking tools encourage healthy debate and allow members to focus on information and not individuals. A good place to start with any team is to define and allocate certain critical roles to its members. This gives them ownership of an important function and a sense that they are valued for a specific contribution to the smooth functioning of the project. Some core roles to assign to different team members at different stages of the project include:

- Timekeeper: This person keeps the project on track and on time. The timekeeper is expected to raise an alarm if things take longer than they should or reports are slow to come in.

- Bookkeeper: This is the treasurer who specifically tracks and reports on financial outlays to estimated costs and budgets.

- Heart keeper: A very important and usually overlooked role. The heart keeper tracks the overall morale and sentiment of the group. This person is a contact point for interpersonal issues within the group and maintains motivation and enthusiasm for the project throughout.

- Stakeholder keeper: The person with this long title maintains relationships with stakeholders and fulfils reporting requirements where applicable.

- Beekeeper: At every meeting someone should be responsible for asking the difficult questions that may well sting a little. This position of *devil's advocate* should be rotated so that everyone has a turn to ensure that critical questions are raised and debate is stimulated at every meeting.

- Record keeper: Once a significant decision has been made, the rationale behind it should be noted or recorded so that it can stand up to examination at a later stage. It doesn't have to include who was in favour of or opposed to the idea or decision. This is an important part of continuously learning how to improve team decisions; through identifying errors in thinking and their consequences.

Depending on the nature of your project and the size of the team, you may need to add or remove some roles.

Cameras, lenses and thinking tools

Everyone on your team might have a different problem-solving approach. This can be time consuming and lead to tension and frustration within the team. What a pity! If teamwork is so powerful because of diversity of ideas, opinions and approaches, how can we turn these frictions into an asset? Team leaders need effective tools to back them up when the going gets tough.

Now try thinking of all the different frames of mind with which you can approach a problem. I have given you four frames of mind to get you started.

How many different frames of mind can you approach a problem with?	
1. positive	2. critical
3. creative	4. systematic
5.	6.
7.	8.

Circle the ones you think are the most important. You might have guessed that the best answer was to circle all of them. Each frame of mind examines a different aspect of the problem.

Quite early in life we learn what decision-making techniques work for us. We tend to stick to these and continually approach problems in the same way. We become very good at using our own technique. There is a danger that this becomes a habit that closes us off from new ideas and perspectives. Thinking tools recognise that we get stuck in a thinking rut. They force us out of our comfort zone, which leads to better decision making individually and in teams.

A formal process that looks at a problem or task through many different frames will yield far more thorough results than basic brainstorming that asks for random ideas to throw into the pot. Let me explain how.

My husband loves photography and has a bewildering array of cameras, lenses and filters that he lugs around in a giant case. Each camera and lens does a different job with remarkably different results. I find the complexity and bulk of all the equipment very off-putting. Tossing my indestructible little point-and-shoot camera into my bag is more my style. However, when we get home after a holiday everyone wants to see *his* photos because they have contrast, depth, artistry and real 'oomph'. My photos are all pretty blah — one dimensional, flat and fairly bland — even though we photographed the same subjects. My hubby's different cameras and lenses all captured a different aspect of what we had seen.

When tackling problems alone, or in a team, one point of view (like my point-and-shoot camera) will never yield the insights and depth needed to perceive every aspect of it with the clarity and diversity needed to generate great solutions. We need four different cameras and at least five different lenses in our backpack to give us an optimal problem-solving strategy. Let's take a closer look at our problem solving equipment.

Firstly, every problem and possible solution must be considered from the viewpoint of each stakeholder. A general guide is:

- Camera 1: the team's point of view

- Camera 2: the company's/other departments' and stakeholders' points of view

- Camera 3: clients' or customers' points of view

- Camera 4: your competitors' points of view

The team's point of view

The company's/other departments' and stakeholders' points of view

Clients' point of view

Your competitors' point of view

Now we can put a different lens on each of the cameras to get a sense of how the problem is viewed by each group through each different lens. This will yield up to 24 different perspectives to be evaluated. I'm sure you will agree this is a pretty thorough investigation of the problem and potential solutions. If all this 'equipment' is too much for your backpack or time you have available, feel free to pick the combinations that are most applicable to your project, but try to keep as many combinations as possible.

Once your cameras are set up, it's time to fit the different lenses on each one.

Lens #1: Lessons

What we know from the past. This includes past successes and failures. Here we would consider what caused these failures or successes and what aspects would be relevant or applicable today?

Lens #2: Assumptions

What we don't know and what assumptions we are making. This includes conventional wisdom, deductions and the status quo. Of course, projections and all aspects that rely on forces beyond our control such as market cycles, sentiment, competitor actions, etc, should be looked at here as well.

Lens #3: Solutions

This is where we use intelligent brainstorming (see Chapter 7) to generate possible solutions.

Lens #4: Risks

What are the dangers of taking on this project? What can go wrong? Scenario analysis will highlight the impact of each of our assumptions if they go according to plan or turn out to be horribly wrong. Each team member should highlight at least one risk. Plugging possible solutions into your system's diagram of the problem will also help everyone in the team *see* the effects of a proposed solution in context.

Lens #5: Resources

What resources do we need and what impact will our project have on other areas of the business? Will we be taking resources away from or will our solution contribute positively to other areas?

Lens #6: Rewards

Do the rewards justify the risks taken? What are the targets or expectations of this project and how certain are we of reaching them?

Lessons

Assumptions

Solutions

Risks

Resources

Rewards

Ten questions to tame the toughest decisions

If you are squeezed for time and have no choice but to examine your problem through only the fixed lens of a point-and-shoot camera, here are ten shortcut questions to get your team thinking clearly.

1. What assumptions are we using in our decision-making process?

2. If any of these assumptions turn out differently from what we imagine, how would the outcome be affected?

3. Could emotions or influences such as frustrations, pride, indifference, lack of motivation, personal agendas and others affect how we approach this problem or the quality of debate?

4. How can we neutralise theses influences upfront?

5. Do I (or the team leader) already have an outcome in mind before I even examine all the facts objectively?

6. Could I (or the team leader) be steering the decision towards my outcome?

7. Have we considered the system in which this problem occurs?

8. What consequences could our decision create for other people/ departments or organisations?

9. If I opposed this project or decision, how would I criticise it?

10. How much flexibility is built into this plan? If our projections or assumptions turn out to be wrong, can we adapt the plan to work towards a different but acceptable outcome?

Star Tips for solving problems in teams

1. Remember that creating teams of individuals that are similar makes for smooth functioning and easy-to-manage teams, but can also result in shallow thinking and poor solutions.

2. Gather a team of diverse individuals. Managing them may be hard but allows for robust problem solving, diverse perspectives and knowledge transfers.

3. Identify any susceptibility that your team might have towards groupthink.

4. Look out for evidence of groupthink developing, especially in highly aligned teams.

5. Beware of assuming that a leader's role is to steer the group towards a certain conclusion.

6. Assign and rotate specific roles to team members to give them accountability for the smooth functioning of the team in addition to their technical input.

7. Ensure healthy debate by using decision-making models that require everybody to offer ideas on possible risks and pitfalls.

8. Examine a problem from the point of view of each stakeholder as well as your competitors using four different cameras.

9. Take your analysis deeper by using six different lenses (lessons, assumptions, solutions, risks, resources and rewards) to get a full and information-rich picture of the issue and solutions at hand.

10. Honour the principles of Ubuntu by remembering that our individuality makes our contribution very valuable to the team, but it is our interconnectedness that makes our team powerful.

CREATING AND SHARING YOUR DECISION-MAKING STRATEGY

10

"You have brains in your head. You have feet in your shoes. You can steer yourself any direction you choose. You're on your own. And you know what you know. And YOU are the one who'll decide where to go..."

Dr. Seuss

Creating your decision-making strategy

There are many different ways to learn something new. As babies we learn the important skill of observation. We see someone do something, decide that it's something we want to learn, then we copy it as best we can. This basic skill remains increasingly important as we grow up and adopt more sophisticated methods of learning. Unfortunately, as we mature, learning through *play* gives way to learning through *pay*. Those who are wealthy enough are able to get what is considered the best education. Ironically, for transferring knowledge, even the best education systems rely on our basic learning process — observe, comprehend and model.

You'll know the mind-numbing agony of an eight-hour *professional training programme* where you are merely expected to sit, listen and comprehend. You may learn more from watching the Disney channel for eight hours. The Disney channel engages more of your senses through sound and pictures.

Now I'm not recommending that you cancel corporate training and switch the TV in the cafeteria from Bloomberg to Little Einsteins (although it could be an interesting exercise). I'm reminding you that reading a book or sitting through two days of training is time well wasted unless you are prepared to dip your toe in the water and experience some of the material through doing so.

I could read about a foreign language obsessively, but unless I speak it, I won't remember it for very long. If I speak it, I'll also get feedback on how much of what I say makes sense, or if my accent is still very odd. No matter how clumsy it feels at first, the only way to internalise new ideas and skills is to externalise them. But learning to think smarter doesn't have to be awkward or painful.

Fast Fact

The only way to internalise a new skill is to externalise it through doing.

Try This

How about taking a chapter every week, or month, and sharing and discussing it with your team? Then practise the principles or even just some of the Star Tips at the end.

Building your decision-making strategy

Now it's your turn. Here's a short summary of the main ideas in this book to jog your memory and to help you plan your own decision-making system.

Education is not our competitive advantage

Our ultimate competitive advantage is our mind's ability to think thoughts that are faster and smarter than our colleagues and competitors. Education is an important component of knowledge, but what we *do* with our knowledge is what sets us apart from our competitors. Reflective thinking is thinking about your past decisions with an eye on identifying both good and bad patterns in your decision-making process.

Over to you: How much time will you devote to thinking about thinking from now on?

Getting on top of information is vital

Information overload and task saturation are not simply buzzwords that will soon make way for the next management craze. Too much information creates confusion, instead of clarity, in our decision making. A healthy information diet that we are always in control of reduces the negative impact of continuous stress. Multitasking makes us feel empowered, valuable… and exhausted! We only have *one* processor (and no, we don't only use 10 per cent of it). We can improve productivity dramatically by unitasking and setting time aside to work uninterrupted.

Over to you. How about committing to unitasking for an hour each day?

Our brain is amazing but it has limited processing power

Ours brains can't process all the sensory input coming at them at once so we delete, distort and generalise information to help us cope. This means that everyone interprets information differently. We all create our own *cover version* of reality. Paraphrasing and reiterating important parts of a conversation help us to check that our understanding is the same as everyone else's.

Over to you: When problem solving, look for opposing opinions before finalising a decision. Ask at least three people, "what am I missing here?" or "what would you do differently?" Free advice that could save you heartache or embarrassment later.

Emotions are an important part of decision making

Emotions are at the core of every decision that we make. We can't change that; it's how we are built. When emotions weigh too heavily in our decisions, it's worth finding out what triggers an excessively emotional response from us by keeping a response diary. This will help us identify rogue emotions. If we can anticipate them we can harness them before they land us in trouble or lead to a poor decision. The *step back skill* and *filler phrases* are tools that supplement our natural ability to use emotions wisely.

Over to you: Keep a response diary for this week.

Mental mistakes 'R' us

We all do it. We unknowingly and unwillingly make mistakes when we process information. If we didn't, decision making would be a breeze and outcomes would be predictable. Presumptions, assumptions, the status quo and conventional wisdom make a tasty cocktail of bad ideas on which to base decisions. They need to be routed out by challenging all assumptions that creep into our decision-making system.

Over to you: Try to spot mental mistakes in your own thinking the next time you wrestle with a challenge.

Being an expert is a high maintenance competitive advantage

Being considered an expert in any field is an achievement. However, it can become a liability when it closes us off from questioning ourselves and being open to new ways of thinking and doing what we do. Remember that challenges evolve in unpredictable ways. Our expertise must be continually updated to consistently meet new challenges.

Over to you: Can you take one action to update your expertise over the next three months?

Manufacturing creativity takes structure and discipline

Great ideas don't just arrive out of nowhere when least expected. Creative solutions are manufactured over time and are usually the result of a conscious or subconscious creative process. Creativity needs fuel, preparation, structure and downtime. A tired, overworked brain will battle to generate brilliant solutions.

Over to you: Do you have a process for generating creative solutions? If you don't, why not draw up a three point plan to create creativity in your thinking?

Complex problems need systematic solutions, not a scalpel

If the problem you are working on is truly a complex problem, then cutting it up to simplify it can cause many of its properties to be lost, leading to poor solutions. Making problems visual by illustrating them with a diagram has multiple benefits. This will highlight differences in viewpoints and understandings while clarifying exactly what the problem is. A system diagram of your problem will show how the problem affects other areas. It will also clarify where the leverage point is. This is where the smallest change will generate the biggest impact. The Gâteau model can help you remember all the elements that should be considered when tackling tricky problems.

Over to you: Visit your art supply store and buy large pieces of paper to allow you to draw systems diagrams of tricky problems.

Teams must be tailored to think together

A team is a problem-solving system. Getting the system working optimally is the only way to repeatedly generate good solutions from it. Teams with members that are very similar in background and outlook can produce great ideas and solutions, but they can also fall foul of groupthink. Diversity in a team can produce robust solutions but only if managed correctly.

Over to you: Which of the several tools in this book can you use to tailor team dynamics towards constructive debate?

So, how will you make better decisions from tomorrow?

Your quick reference checklist

There is no such thing as a one-size-fits-all thinking, decision-making or problem-solving strategy. I certainly couldn't expect anyone to adopt every measure I've suggested in this book. However, if we don't actively design and build our own unique way of approaching problems, then we'll simply fall back on our subconscious processes.

At this point I'm going to stop talking for a bit and give you the opportunity to pen the process that you think will work best for you.

Go back to the Star Tips at the end of each chapter, as well as the summary above, and pick out those ideas that will help you think smart and work smarter from today:

My problem-solving and decision-making checklist
1.
2.
3.
4.
5.
6.
7.
8.
9.
10.

This cheat sheet will help you check that your thinking and conclusions are the best that they could possibly be before you make a decision. Tear it out and keep it in your drawer or pin it up on your notice board.

Changing the way we think is a pretty big deal but it's not as hard to do as you may imagine. Some of the principles of Kaizen[12] are particularly useful and worth remembering when embarking on any kind of change, especially something like this, which involves changing a habit or belief. The Japanese philosophy of Kaizen focuses on creating small but continuous improvements throughout a system. It keeps an eye on steadily tweaking processes and not results. This recognises that a system does what it is programmed to do. There is no such thing as a failing system. In order to change the output or result of the system, the programming must change. My favourite piece of wisdom from this philosophy is that there is *no such thing as perfection*. We should aim for perfection but not expect it.

Communicating your conclusions to others

This isn't a book on how to improve your communication skills. However, it would be a shame if you were unable to effectively communicate the results that you have generated through a great thinking, decision-making or problem-solving process. It would be great if we could summarise our conclusion in a report, send it off to management or our client and receive a *yes* or *no* to our proposal some time later. Unfortunately it rarely works like this. Creating what we believe to be great solutions is only half the battle won. Thereafter we usually need to convince other parties to buy in to our solution. This can be especially challenging when an issue has to be presented in an open forum and laid bare to criticism.

If you are someone who wilts when under pressure or in the spotlight, here are some ideas that might help you communicate your message in the boardroom.

---

12 Kaizen was originally a process improvement and quality control training programme introduced to restore Japan's productivity after WWII and has grown in popularity and practice since then.

Make your solution as visual as possible

This doesn't mean sticking up slide after slide of complicated spaghetti diagrams or dense paragraphs. Choose high-level systems diagrams that show the problem and your solution in context. Don't be afraid of abandoning PowerPoint. As you know it favours bullet points and can be very limiting when it comes to more sophisticated ideas. Diagrams also take some pressure off you, as they will help you remember the content of your presentation much more easily than a row of bullet points.

Anticipate queries, questions and concerns

You know someone will raise them. If you've looked at the problem through four different cameras and at least a couple of different lenses, you should be prepared for a range of questions from most stakeholders. If you need to disagree with someone's viewpoint, show him or her why by referring to the diagram.

Be careful not to fall in love with your solution

Your team might have missed something. New solutions might come from the audience or become evident in later discussions. It is very tempting to dismiss critical ideas. Let's face it, being challenging by an audience member when you are on the spot presenting an idea, is a lot for any ego to handle. Part of being an expert and a good thinker is the ability to accept and integrate new information in your thinking. When all eyes are on you, how you handle opposition can influence how others perceive you.

Present a very thorough scenario analysis

Try to paint an accurate picture with both the upside and the downside. Show that you have considered the issues from different perspectives. If you don't, the audience may test you on it.

Lastly, if you know you have used a thorough process to generate ideas or solutions, you will have gained a very deep understanding of the issue at hand and its effects on other areas. This should instill confidence in your ability to cope with curveballs, challenging audience members and critical clients. Take a deep breath and smile; it's good for you.

Aha! Moment

If I have used a very thorough process to investigate an issue, I can feel confident when presenting my ideas to an audience. I may not have thought of everything, but will have a very deep understanding of the issues involved. This will help me deal with tricky questions.

Empowering others to think smart, work smarter

Once you have discovered the power and benefits of thinking and working smarter, you may well want to spread your newfound knowledge and empower colleagues to make better decisions and work smarter as well. When I first started down the road of training 'critical thinking', as it is called in organisations today, I was intrigued by the resistance that I initially received from those who paid me to coach them in improving their decision-making skills. I realised, after some time, that I wasn't offering them a pill to pop or a quick fix solution. Senior executives, and everyone else, may be uncomfortable having their mental mistakes exposed or their emotional responses examined. Most of us don't want to learn a whole new skill set when our university days are well and truly behind us. Experts don't want to hear that expertise is a renewable label! Even if they know it's true.

Fast Fact

Age is guaranteed, wisdom is not.

However, this knowledge is so powerful and important in changing the financial and strategic futures of companies and governments, their leaders and workers that I couldn't give up. I just had to get a lot smarter in how I offered this information. I learnt to use guerrilla tactics to explain and illustrate the principles of critical thinking, and I haven't looked back.

Mental mistakes are introduced by allowing participants to experience making the mental mistake first. This proves that they are susceptible to each and every one of them. When you notice colleagues, and even family members, making mental mistakes, it may be best to let the mistakes happen and then offer solutions. Once people *see* the benefits of processing information better, and understand that we are able to change our factory fitted software that controls how we think, they become much more open to considering the tools suggested.

Tread lightly around emotions in decisions, because many people take time to warm up to this idea. Especially if they pride themselves on being 100 per cent rational in everything they do. I have learnt never to tell anyone anything, but to use questioning and a coaching approach to help individuals understand the emotions that are bundled into our decisions. "How does it make you *feel?*" is an interesting alternative to asking, "what do you think of that?" and "how did you come to that conclusion?"

Of course, the best way is to lead by example and make everyone curious as to the secrets of your success. Remember to give them something to observe, help them understand and then let them try it out for themselves.

Fast Fact

Yesterday's decisions create today's reality. Today's decisions create our future.

Star Tips for creating and sharing your decision-making strategy

1. Remember that learning anything new relies on our basic learning skills of seeing, understanding and doing.

2. Design and build your own unique way of approaching problems by completing the problem-solving and decision-making checklist on page 176. This will help you avoid simply falling back on your subconscious processes.

3. Tear your checklist out and keep it where you do most of your thinking. Think about your thinking every day.

4. Use the principles of Kaizen by creating small but continuous process improvements in your thinking.

5. Remember that there is no such thing as a failing system because a system produces only what it is programmed to create.

6. Make your solutions as visual as possible when presenting them to help your audience understand them better.

7. Anticipate queries, questions and concerns, and don't fall in love with your solution, no matter how hot it is!

8. Be confident when presenting your solutions. If you have used a very thorough approach to creating it, you would have gained great insights into the material and could probably deal with most questions on it.

9. Help others to think and work smarter by showing them solutions to address stumbling blocks in their thinking process.

10. Share, never tell. You'll be glad you did.

INDEX

ABOUT THE AUTHOR

Tremaine du Preez is a leadership coach and head of learning and development for The Leadership Consultancy, a boutique coaching and training consultancy based in Singapore.

Originally from Cape Town, South Africa, she has developed an approach to leadership and human capital development that fuses the best of Eastern, Western and African ideas. She is a sought after trainer and speaker in strategic management, emotional intelligence and critical thinking, and offers a rich depth of knowledge in these areas.

Participants who attend her workshops on critical thinking continually inspire her to find new, and fun, ways of making academic and high level ideas as accessible as possible. She firmly believes that everyone should benefit from the research and advances in mankind's understanding of how to use our minds to their full potential.

Tremaine has a master's degree in Financial Economics from the University of London, a Bachelor of Commerce in Informatics and is certified in Neuro-Semantics. She has lived in Asia for seven years, and works throughout the region helping senior executives, government officials and other leaders develop their leadership, problem-solving and decision-making skills.

Find out more about Tremaine at www.leadershipconsultancy.org

 **ST Training Solutions**

Success Skills Series

ST Training Solutions, based in Singapore, offers a wide range of popular, practical training programmes conducted by experienced, professional trainers. As CEO, Shirley Taylor takes a personal interest in working closely with trainers to ensure that each workshop is full of valuable tools, helpful guidelines and powerful action steps that will ensure a true learning experience for all participants. Some of the workshops offered are:

Powerful Business Writing Skills
Energise your E-mail Writing Skills
Success Skills for Secretaries and Support Staff
Successful Business Communication Skills
Building Great Business Relationships
Creativity at Work
Speaking without Fear
Professional People Skills
Writing Back to Customers Effectively
Win-Win Negotiation Skills
Emotional Intelligence at Work
Grammar Gold
Dealing with Difficult People and Situations
Achieving Peak Performance by Improving your Memory
Master Your Minute Writing

Shirley Taylor is also host of a very popular annual conference called ASSAP — the Asian Summit for Secretaries and Admin Professionals — organised in April each year by ST Training Solutions.

Find out more about ST Training Solutions at www.shirleytaylortraining. com. Visit www.STSuccessSkills.com for additional resources.